WHAT OTHERS ARE SAYING

"This is a book that everybody should have when they leave school at the age of 18. It is a financial literacy book. It not only teaches you from the financial perspective on making money but also from the perspective of what kind of person you need be to create wealth. Wealth and assets are different things. Wealth and net worth are also different things. Also, from a female perspective, I connected with the book."

—Kristina Nyzell, Co-Founder of *Futureproof Fund,*
Founder and CEO of *Disruptiveplay,*
Board Member Women for Sustainable Growth (W4SG.ORG)

"In his book, The Wealth of Generations, Mr. Anderson tackles a vital subject and gives us the chance to get ahead of it before it may be too late— our ability to earn wealth. While we do not know exactly what the future may hold, we can definitely look at current trends and where we may be headed in society over the next hundred years. The things we learn now and can pass on to our kids and grandchildren may mean the difference in their ability to thrive in a rapidly changing economy. This book is a very important read."

—Adam C. Smith, Devotee of *"The Wealth of Nations"*

The Wealth Of Generations is a comprehensive wealth study guide of colossal proportions with three Parts covering more than 30 topics on success growth and the common facts, most of which elude those with no interest in wealth and finances.

Every great book starts and ends with the authors, publishers, and any team players behind it, so this is one where I give credit to everyone involved. It is especially worth complimenting and of the main reason to recommend this book with flying colors. A lot went into making it a solid study and reference book without boring the reader, which is essential for any book's effort's to last. So, the first word goes to Ingemar Anderson for an excellent product.

Part one starts with Morals: and Why Leave A Legacy is the first question, so if you haven't read this book and want significant insight from one review, don't skip anything, and you'll get the most out of *The Wealth of Generations*.

*The book explains the Seven Investor Levels and the Division of Labor. It gets more and more interesting as it passes through Part two with the Mindset of an Investor, Types of Asset Classes, Why Does Wealth Only Trickle Up, and the State of Wealth altogether.

Anderson saved the best for last with Part three taking the prize for the gauntlet of information and topic variation in *The Wealth of Generations*. That is where the credit adds up and goes to anyone else behind the work done to deliver this title. The details are tremendous, and the facts are astounding in this well-written book. And to top it off, the book ends with Family Wealth—My Grandfather's Story.

—**Trace Whittaker,** *Reprospace Editorial Reviews™*

THE WEALTH OF GENERATIONS

Transitioning from Nation-Centered Capitalism to Human-Centered Capitalism and a Shared Economy

Ingemar Anderson

KITSAP

PUBLISHING

The Wealth of Generations
First Edition, Published 2020

By Ingemar Anderson

Cover Design and Interior Layout by Reprospace, LLC
Cover Photo by Visualarts, Croatia

Copyright © 2020, Ingemar Anderson

Hardcover ISBN-13: 978-1-952685-05-7
Paperback ISBN-13: 978-0-989455-12-1

This book contains information about financial firms and their products and services such as real estate, stocks, bonds, and other types of investments. While this book is intended to provide information on financial matters and investments, such information or references should not be construed or interpreted as investment advice or viewed as an endorsement. The author has invested and likely will invest in the products and services discussed in this book. However, any comments or suggestions offered in this book regarding such financial firms or their products and services are solely the opinions of the author.

20201028 987654321

Published by
Kitsap Publishing
P.O. Box 572
Poulsbo, WA 98370
www.KitsapPublishing.com

Dedication

I dedicate this book to my grandfather, Per Ingemar Aae, and to my son Benjamin.

My grandfather's life ended tragically at the young age of 34 after suffering for several months before he died from leukemia.

During the Great Depression in the 1930s, he was sent to the United States from Sweden to help large struggling companies implement accounting and fiscal statements. He brought his knowledge and experience back to Sweden, where he became a university professor to teach finance and accounting.

I hope that future generations of my now teenage son will benefit from this book. I believe that the book follows my grandfather's footsteps and continues the work that he was never able to complete.

Acknowledgments

Because of my family and friends, I am a wealthy person. No, I am not talking about inheriting or receiving a lot of money from my friends or family. Their integrity, wisdom, and commitment have given me more than money can buy. I received love, wisdom, knowledge, morals, and they encouraged me to write this book.

I want to thank my dad, who always looked out for me and inspired me with his sincere, loving, and beautiful mind. I thank my mother for her unbreakable braveness and toughness, which taught me many lessons in life. My younger brother and sister went very different paths in their lives than I did but always had a significant influence on me and made me a better person.

Robert, my dear friend in middle school shared my early dreams of space travel and investing. My friend Peter in highschool inspired me with his brilliant musical compositions, entrepreneurial spirit, and writing talents.

My dear college friends Kurt and Markus, taught me to take care of my mind and body. I will never forget our breathtaking hiking and biking tours in the German, Austrian and Swiss Alps.

I thank all my friends, colleagues, professors, business partners, customers, and teachers in my career and during my Executive MBA program: Raimund, Tasos, Mark, Hans, Paul, Ira, Velimir, Susan, Adam, Tim, Michael, Thomas, Harald, Becky, Rosie, Christina, John, Kevin, Horst, Tom, Sheila, Puja, Alexander, and Mike who all shared their sincere friendship and their profound minds with me as software programmers, pastors, medical doctors, financial advisors, asset managers, mayors, business owners, business consultants, bookkeepers, real estate brokers, contractors, lawyers, entrepreneurs, and CEOs. They made me the person that I am today.

Finally, and most influential in my life are my wife and my son Benjamin. My son's hunger to learn, his brilliant minds, and positive energy have given me the final push to finish this book.

Ingemar Alexander Anderson

CONTENTS

*The Thinker, adapted from the original bronze sculpture by Auguste Rodin.
Illustration by Ingemar Anderson.*

Introduction

"I don't want a nation of thinkers. I want a nation of workers."

—John D. Rockefeller, 1903

About a hundred years ago, our society became officially a nation of workers when the *General Education Board*, funded by John D. Rockefeller in 1902, announced its mission to support higher education in the United States with presumably good intentions to build a nation of workers. But today, stagnating income from labor is leaving an army of employees with little to no room to grow lasting wealth.

Why? Because our current capitalistic system's dirty little secret is that, over time, capital tends to grow by several percentage points faster than salaries and wages. So, people working for money have been losing the race to building wealth and will always lose against those who use financial capital to create wealth.

The gap between the small minority of people who leverage capital to build wealth and workers is growing bigger each year. Spurred by technological advances, this trend is now even accelerating, and the value of skilled labor is declining to unsustainable levels.

Consequently, our century-old democracy seems to turn into an oligarchy. Then, power would rest with a small number of people distinguished by nobility, wealth, education, corporate, religious, political, or military control. Our society would then be controlled by families who pass their influence from one generation to the next. Is this what we want?

THE VALUE OF SKILLED LABOR

Today, the fundamental principle of capitalism, the concept of skilled labor, is at stake. Is it possible that we can all pass wealth from one generation to another? Can we manage a paradigm shift from nation-centered capitalism to a shared economy based on the Wealth of Generations by enabling all workers to become capitalists—sophisticated investors? The answer is yes! This book casts a positive outlook into the future by suggesting using artificial intelligence and other technologies to make us all capitalists, reaping equitable returns.

Studies claim a 100% chance of Artificial Intelligence (AI) replacing all human tasks by somewhere between 2060 and 2200.[1] More importantly, these studies also reveal that this process has already started today and is ahead of every prediction. AI built into services like aitranslate.com are already translating languages, which specialists expected to happen by 2024, and apps like aiva.ai already create professionally composed music. The newest AI-supported applications can already write essays, which was predicted to occur in 2026. In 2021, AI is driving trucks on our highways, which was estimated to happen in 2027. What's next? Retail salespersons, authors of novels and non-fiction books—the list is long and frightening. Many studies predict that AI will write bestselling books by 2049, and AI will work as a surgeon by 2053.

This book will discuss options for preparing us for an emerging job market collapse and building wealth for generations in a world without the need for skilled labor, transitioning our economy from nation-centered capitalism to human-centered capitalism.

---

1   *"When Will AI Exceed Human Performance? Evidence from AI Experts," Future of Humanity Institute, Oxford University, AI Impacts, Department of Political Science, Yale University (https://arxiv.org/pdf/1705.08807.pdf)*

For three centuries, since the birth of modern capitalism, ignited by Adam Smith's book *"The Wealth of Nations"* in 1776, the general belief is that the desired way to make money is to get a job and sell our skilled labor to corporations and their helpers—the nation's governments. But today, with technology claiming more and more of our jobs, this paradigm starts to fail us since emerging technologies get the work done faster, better, and cheaper.

This book will explore why our generation is in danger of becoming less empowered in our current capitalistic model due to an ever-shrinking value of skilled human labor. I will describe why our current form of capitalism will fail us if we do not make a fundamental adjustment, switching from nation-centered capitalism to a human-centered and decentralized capitalistic model.

The gap between the *rich* and the *poor* could widen to unsustainable levels. And with every new economic down-turn, this gap seems to worsen. In *Figure 1a*, later in this introduction, a graph shows data provided by the Federal Reserve's research group that hints at the reason for this development: *the value of skilled labor is falling significantly relative to productivity increases since the 1990s due to technological advances.* The fundamental idea of capitalism, skilled labor, is at stake.

In my book, I will explore remedies for replacing human skills with technology, driven by artificial intelligence (AI), robots, and technologies like blockchain. The newest OpenAI GPT release (Generative Pre-trained Transformer) and other emerging technologies can be terrifying. Technology is starting to threaten reputable occupations like software developers, lawyers, journalists, and editors. For example, I am writing the text, which you are reading right now, using an AI-powered writing enhancement tool called Grammarly.

Since the beginning of humankind, we have continuously improved our mental and practical skills, and we applied them to make a living. With the appearance of this new breed of technology, we might face a terrible realization: we, as humans, are no longer the only ones who can learn and perfect a skill anymore. We knew that we would lose control of this technological development one day. Have we reached the *technological singularity*, the point where technological growth is becoming uncontrollable and irreversible with unforeseeable changes to our human civilization?

Some of us might feel already how these advances in technology affect our personal and professional lives? Technological improvements have already changed the way how we make money. Machines *'think'* and *'work'* faster than humans, have more endurance and are less emotionally attached to decisions. This time, it is for real. With new developments in AI and blockchain applications hitting the market every day, the meaning of work is changing for all of us and forever.

What implications does the singularity have on the way we make money and provide for our loved ones? How can we prepare ourselves? Let's start at the beginning of modern capitalism.

The Scottish 17th-century economist and pioneer of political economy is the author of the book *"The Wealth of Nations,"* published in 1776. He is known as *"The Father of Economics"* or *"The Father of Capitalism."* His book is driven by the idea of the division of labor and industrial productivity. It is considered an *"Inquiry into the Nature and Causes of the Wealth of Nations."*

In contrast, this book in your hands is an *Inquiry into the Nature and Causes of the Wealth of Generations* and focuses on making us, the people, more wealthy.

For centuries, the wealth of nations has risen dramatically, country by country, led by various governments and huge mega-corporations that have often turned into monstrous money machines. This trend has been propelled by The *General Education Board*, founded in 1902 after John D. Rockefeller donated an initial one million dollars to its cause. The board's mission was to emphasize the need for real-world applicational skills like *Demonstrative Farming* and *Industrial Education*.

Since then, our school system mostly ignored practical financial education and teaching a systematic approach to building personal wealth. The book in your hands elaborates on fundamental principles and financial knowledge to building generational wealth.

Let's look back in history. While nations grew richer, only a tiny proportion of us became wealthy. In contrast, founders of these mega-corporations, kings in the past centuries, and sophisticated investors today became free from working for money. For most of us, it has been, at best, a comfortable ride. As a matter of fact, the vast majority of people and their families today cannot be considered wealthy. Quite the opposite, it seems that families are mostly burdened by mountains of debt and little time for creativity. And the trend got worse since the *Great Recession in 2008*.

This book, *The Wealth of Generations*, is written for us, the people, the *working* people, it is written for us, humans! It explains in layman's terms why it is essential for everyone to build wealth for generations and how everyone can do it. Today's financial education is mainly based on how we can make nations and corporations richer by giving in to the division of labor and over-specialization, while being compartmentalized in the anonymous machinery, only to achieve mediocre financial successes for ourselves. The goal of this book is to describe how we can create genuine wealth to achieve freedom for generations.

WHAT'S WEALTH?

Simply put, wealth is *leverage*. No, not leverage like in the world of physics as the exertion of force using a lever or an object applied in the manner of a lever. No, also not the ratio of loaned capital (debt) to the value of its equity.

Leverage in the sense of influence. We can have *moral* influence, *knowledge-based* influence, and influence through *money*. Leverage enables us to move things forward—for ourselves and others. When we have enough leverage, we are free to create our future. Financial wealth exists in many forms. The terms capital and assets are essential to this book. So, buckle up!

Most people underestimate that being wealthy involves a lot of work and that wealth is the ultimate business no matter how large it is. Wealth is a combination of sufficient capital and the freedom and knowledge to deploy it. Ergo, wealth comes with responsibility, and someone needs to manage wealth, or it will disappear over time.

But the definition and symbols of wealth change over time. For example, kings used to wear purple clothes to demonstrate their wealth. For centuries, people associated the color purple with royalty, power, and wealth. Queen Elizabeth I did not allow anyone except close members of the royal family to wear it. The elite status of the color purple stems from the dye's scarcity and cost to produce it.

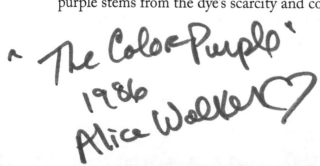

"The Color Purple"
1986
Alice Walker

DECENTRALIZED WEALTH

Wealth Management is the planning and control of capital and its related transactions. An entire industry has evolved based on the need to plan and allocate people's and company assets.

A large portion of wealth management is the settlement of contracts offered as a service by wealth managers in small and large financial firms. But one technology is now changing everything: blockchain. This new technology is transforming financial institutions and consequently transforms wealth management in itself. Blockchain is an open, distributed ledger that can authenticate assets and people's identity and record transactions between two parties reliably in a verifiable way.

Blockchain is already reducing or eliminating the need for banks and governmental bureaucracy, increasing the audibility and trust between parties. Blockchain can help shape a more efficient health-care system, detect academic fraud, create a better banking experience, provide a more efficient humanitarian aid distribution system, or help companies avoid personal data breaches.

Why is this important? It matters because blockchain is changing the way we build wealth. The meaning of wealth might even change completely. For example, today, bitcoin is the most used application of this new blockchain technology. Bitcoin is a drastic new way to store and transfer value. Unlike traditional financial networks, bitcoin can operate without central authorities or trusted administrators. That makes bitcoin the first-ever open and borderless quasi-currency. I have regularly invested in bitcoin as the price rose by over 80,000 percent after its inception in 2009. Today, the easiest way to buy and sell bitcoins is by using smartphone apps like Cash App.

WHAT DO I MEAN BY GENERATIONS?

To me, generations are groups of people who live on this planet at a particular time. These groups can be families or larger populations like tribes, people who affiliate with a specific trend or are just part of an era in time. Millennials or baby-boomers belong to their generations. By generations, I also mean groups of people that live during different times but are related. For example, farmers hand their businesses over from one generation to the next. We might view the term generations as a two-dimensional expression covering space and time: different generations who live together today in one space and new generations will take on their generation's heritage.

WHAT IS SKILLED LABOR?

Investopia.com defines skilled labor as "... *a segment of the workforce that has specialized know-how, training, and experience to carry out more complex physical or mental tasks than routine job functions.*"

Let's look at a definition of another term. The University of Minnesota writes, "... *Artificial Intelligence (AI) ... is a general term that implies the use of a computer to model and replicate intelligent behavior. Research in AI focuses on developing and analyzing algorithms that learn and perform intelligent behavior with minimal human intervention.*"

So, having "*specialized know-how to carry out more complex physical or mental tasks*" sounds to me like "*learning and performing intelligent behavior with minimal ... intervention.*"

We saw it coming: skilled labor is at the peril of being taken over entirely by artificial intelligence. A project run by OpenAI has developed an AI model called GPT, which stands for "*Generative Pre-training Transformer.*" It is a language model that generates world knowledge by training on vast amounts of texts. Today, AI can already write novels, poetry, provide legal services, computer programming, and drive a car without any human intervention on a level never seen before.

The carmaker Tesla, for example, is rolling out its first fully self-driving cars in the late 2021s. These cars turn into robotaxis, which removes the human driver completely. Implications for truck drivers and taxi companies are colossal. The question is not if AI will take over all skilled labor, but when the transition to a world without the need for skilled labor will be complete.

It becomes clear to me that we, as a society, need to start redefining the skilled-labor paradigm and begin exploring the *nature and causes of the wealth of generations* in a world without the need for skilled labor.

WHERE DOES WEALTH COME FROM?

Imagine a sprinting race where some runners get a head-start of several steps? Would you be surprised if these runners arrive first at a 100 meters sprint? (Watch https://youtu.be/ZZuucE4R65Q)

The title of this book, *The Wealth of Generations*, addresses this very problem by proposing a solution rather than merely pointing out or dwelling upon social inequality. It tries to explain why many people live in impoverishment for generations, are tied hand and foot to the wage economy while others can leverage their efforts through a wealth of morals, mind, and money. *Spiritual* Capital, *Intellectual* Capital, and *Financial* Capital are designed to generate wealth. Wealth is essentially a generator of more wealth because profits can be reinvested to yield more capital, hence more wealth to its owners and beneficiaries.

Today, *information* is the one "*commodity*" that can be used over and over again without being depleted. That is why we are living at a time when more people than ever before are finding that they can generate resources that will outlast the needs of those who have created them. Human progress depends upon this surplus of ideas and physical structures, which can be passed on to new generations.

MERCANTILISM—CAPITALISM—WELTHISM?

Between the 1500s and 1700s, as a way to make money, people were mainly trading goods. This system was called *Mercantilism*, and it was built on the idea to make money when purchasing goods in one region and selling them in another province for more money to make a profit.

In the mid-1700s, however, when nations formed and Adam Smith's work *The Wealth of Nations* became known, *Capitalism* became the new prevalent economic system. This new paradigm has been based on the division of labor to create value by processing goods and material. The idea of modern manufacturing was born. Now, the economic system was driven by two forces: trade and a labor-intensive component to create value and profits.

Today, this capitalistic system has created groups of individuals and families who became ultra-rich, ultra-wealthy. This same system has also created an army of workers and employees with some financial freedom but neglectable wealth. However, we have seen the gap between rich and poor grow for many decades. This new phenomenon has been first described by Joanie Bronfman, who originally coined a new term *Wealthism* in her 1987 doctoral dissertation at Brandeis University. Today, we can see *Wealthism* as a system where wealth is the fundamental factor of prosperity, whereas financial differences between classes create enormous tensions between wealthy and poor people.

Mercantilism and *capitalism* have brought unseen freedom and wealth to many. However, these economic systems are based on the assumption that humans can participate in that system by providing labor. This paradigm is changing today. The rate of technological progress is starting to exceed human abilities to adapt and to compete. This process will end with the result that all (labor-intensive) work can be done by technology.

CAPITAL VS. LABOR

In classical economics, *factors of production* are what is used in the production process to produce output (finished goods and services).

There are two types of *factors of production*: primary and secondary. The three primary factors are:

- Land,
- Labor (human capital),
- Capital.

Secondary factors in classical economics are materials and energy because they are obtained from land, labor, and capital.

The primary factors facilitate production, but neither become part of the product (like raw materials) nor become significantly transformed by the production process (like fuel used to power machinery). Land includes not only the site of production but also natural resources above or below the soil.

Only recently, economists started to distinguish between human capital and labor. They now recognize human capital as the stock of knowledge in the labor force. This distinction illustrates a significant trend that seems to be the start of a more considerable change in understanding the economic system. No longer is labor defined as mere humans' work, but human *knowledge* becomes a significant production factor.

With a nearing technological *intelligence explosion*[2] propelled by artificial intelligence and robot technologies, is it possible that technology can replace both human capital and labor entirely in the next economic revolution? In that scenario, is it possible that the new primary factors of production should be as follows:

- Land,
- *Machine Labor*,
- Capital?

WEALTH WITHOUT WORK

The concept of getting paid for skilled work is entirely based on the assumption that only humans can perform professional work (paid work).

But robots exponentially improve their intellectual capabilities, dexterity, and fine motor control and compete with skilled human workers' hands. They can now mimic the dynamic capabilities of human motion and deal with unpredictability. These increasing capabilities will ultimately also enable robots to maintain and repair themselves completely.

This trend is why skilled labor jobs are not safe from the robot *apocalypse*. Robots and artificial intelligence (AI) are cheaper, faster, and have more endurance than humans.

So, how will ordinary people be able to create wealth in the future? What will be our purpose? The only way to survive the robot *apocalypse* is to put a fleet of robots to work before they put *us* to work.

---

2 *Intelligence explosion is a possible outcome of humanity building artificial general intelligence (AGI). AGI would be capable of recursive self-improvement, leading to the rapid emergence of artificial superintelligence (ASI), the limits of which are unknown, shortly after technological singularity is achieved. I. J., Reference: https:// en.wikipedia.org/wiki/Technological_singularity.*

The trend of the last centuries has been that the overall sophistication of workers has risen dramatically. Today, high-skilled office jobs have become the norm rather than the exception. This book's basic idea is to elaborate on this trend by suggesting that people should accept the concept of *machine labor* and put this emerging army of robots to work to create wealth. Here are just some simple ideas:

- The company Tesla offers a smartphone app that allows car owners to put their cars into a *robotaxi* fleet. Their vehicles can then be used as taxis, driving passengers autonomically from point A to point B and making money for the vehicle owner.
- Many truck drivers already operate their own diesel trucks and drive them to deliver goods to make money. In the human-centered economy, truck drivers can now invest in one or more a self-driving electric trucks and build a fleet of self-driving trucks to make money.
- Solar roofs. It is easier than ever to put electricity generated by solar back into the public power grid and make money by selling electricity.
- What about providing content? Many entrepreneurs are creating intellectual property (IP) and offering access to it on the web. Many famous writers already make a living by selling their work on, for example, *Substack.com*.
- You can train cooking robots and open a restaurant. The *Spyce Restaurant* in Boston is the first restaurant with a robotic kitchen. The owners employ only a small team who prepares the ingredients in an off-site kitchen. Robots do all of the actual cooking. A video on YouTube shows its operation.
- Today, writing a book and receiving royalty payments is also a way to earn passive income using AI. I wrote this book with the support of an AI-supported editing app called *Grammarly*. Furthermore, I distribute my book using a blockchain-driven publishing platform for digital distribution and a physical

book distributor, which uses a fully automated distribution system from order processing to shipping.

- YouTubers: well-known names like *PewDiePie, Shane Dawson,* and *Smosh* earn millions by uploading videos on YouTube and forming personal relationships with their fans.
- Each of us has assets that we can share with others. You can use Airbnb.com to rent out your living space to other people, or use apps like Neighbor.com to rent out your storage space.

People are using smart, emerging technology, driven partly by AI to generate a scalable income, in many cases in the form of passive income—meaning the hours they spend are not directly related to the money they make.

But a world without paid labor is not utopia, an imagined place in which everything is perfect. A solid moral foundation, a sense of purpose and belonging to solve existential problems become the center of our existence. More than ever, we need politicians with sound principles and businesses that promote morality, science that reflects humanity, a technology that considers ethics, an economy that includes sustainability, and knowledge from character.

VOLUNTEER WORK

Volunteer work is an essential concept of *The Wealth of Generations*. With an increasing number of sophisticated investors, people have more time to help others in need. Retirees and other groups of people already offer their work in organizations like Rotaries and other non-profit organizations. Also, many people might not like to be opportunists and leverage machine labor to make money. Therefore, future sophisticated investors should have a unique and vital new civic duty to support these individuals in our society for the common good.

THE RATE OF CHANGE

Ever since technological evolution started, the rate of improvement has been growing exponentially. For example, Moore's Law originated around 1970 and states that processor speeds or overall processing power for computers will double every two years. That is exponential growth. It was proven correct for the past decades—even though the speed of processor improvement has slowed down somewhat in recent years due to technological limitations of materials used to make processors, growth on average is exponential over a longer time.

Human progress, in general, appears to be exponential. In general, we can observe accelerating progress in technological change throughout history, suggesting a faster and more profound rate of change in the future and may or may not be accompanied by equally profound social and cultural change.

Ray Kurzweil calls this phenomenon *The Law of Accelerating Returns*. On his website kurzweil.net, he states that *"technological change is exponential, contrary to the common-sense 'intuitive linear' view. So we won't experience 100 years of progress in the 21st century—it will be more like 20,000 years of progress (at today's rate). The 'returns,' such as chip speed and cost-effectiveness, also increase exponentially."*

Past technological improvements have taken many jobs, and many new job categories have been created. People were able to adapt, relearn new skills, and find new employment in areas that technology could not replace yet.

But what if the rate of technological improvements surpasses the maximum speed of how fast people can change their careers? This moment in time has silently started three decades ago. Since 1990, productivity has increased by 70 percent, whereas salaries and wages only increased by 20 percent. This trend is accelerating. Today, many truck drivers will soon lose their jobs to self-driving semis, and taxi drivers are losing their jobs to robotaxis. Progress always prefers less expensive and more efficient solutions. And this time, employees are not challenged to learn just a new job. This time, they will need to adapt to an entirely new lifestyle and become sophisticated investors.

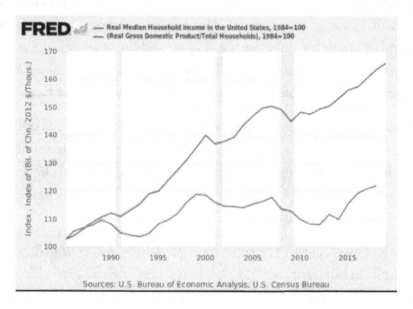

Figure 1a Household Income vs. U.S. Productivity based on fred.stlouisfed.org

In other words, skilled labor performed by humans is becoming less and less valuable. This trend is the reason why the average household is becoming poorer. The wealth of nations is rising, whereas the wealth of people goes down. Karl Marx must have been right in one thing: *capitalism has always meant a struggle between capital and labor.*

I wrote this book for people who want to start replacing their earned income partly or entirely with income from capital. I envision that we all become sophisticated investors who work for free, using tangible and intangible capital to create more capital. I predict that *poor people will keep working for money, whereas sophisticated investors will use technology as the ultimate wealth creation tool.*

This book attempts to shed light on the fundamental concepts of generational wealth creation, a subject that has never been taught in school. It will prepare you for the emerging *technological singularity* by exploring options to deploy your skills in a drastically changing labor market.

The approaching technological singularity can be a scary moment in time. But we should always remember that to love is the one human ability that can not be replaced by technology or anything else. Love is the most powerful force in the universe. And as Ira Kaufman and Velimir Srića write in their book *EmPower Us!*: *"Love is the secret human weapon that will out-think machines and drive progress."*

In 2020, we have seen what a global COVID-19 pandemic can do to our economy, and we have experienced a different reality at work and in our homes. Many of us have made permanent changes to our lives to focus more on family and friends. We have started to re-focus on *The Wealth of our Generations*.

Part One of this book evaluates our morals that are required to build wealth. *Part Two* describes the investor's mind, and *Part Three* explains the money-related portion of wealth.

Foreword

I left my twenty-year career as a high-payed business consultant at one of the top-five consultancy firms in 2008. Ever since, I started four companies, invested in several real estate properties for income and capital gain, and I traded commodities and securities with much success as my only occupation. During that time, I accumulated assets worth more than 30 years of an average worker, and I can now cover my expenses from my assets' income.

My choice to leave my conventional career in 2008 as an employee had many causes. The apparent reason was that I wanted to be available for my new-born son. I also started to have ethical concerns with some company policies regarding travel and other long-term strategies. My biggest problem, however, was that I missed following my passion. In my job, I felt compartmentalized and over-specialized. I wanted to secure my family's future not only from a monetary perspective. My 401(k) retirement account would have been much more worth today than my current asset portfolio. However, I would have missed over a decade of learning how to become a sophisticated investor. Now, I have an excellent financial basis and much experience in investing in all five basic asset classes: *real estate, commodities, securities, money market, and businesses.*

With new technologies like artificial intelligence, robots, and blockchain replacing many of our jobs, we should all learn how to manage capital. The gap between rich and poor is growing bigger unless the average employees and workers are willing to spend more time becoming financially literate and sophisticated investors.

PART ONE

MORALS

CHAPTER 1

Why leave a Legacy?

"The faith of the human race is more than ever dependent on its moral strength today." —Albert Einstein

Why should anyone leave a legacy? I will attempt to answer this preliminary question before all else with some of my thoughts in the form of twenty-three simple bullet points and then discuss them further.

- All of the human progress is predicated on a legacy of knowledge and upon leaving a capital base to finance further growth.
- The span of each human life is relatively short and, as such, does not always allow adequate time to go through each of the necessary stages of complex development of ideas and the means to execute them.
- In evolutionary time to stand still, is already to be outmoded.
- Success and just social competition for future generations require roughly even starting points to begin with a legacy of wealth in values, education, and capital.
- To depend on a mere chance to provide a competitive edge is wishful thinking.
- To imagine that hardship for its own sake breeds moral character rather than exhaustion and demoralization merely is erroneous.
- To compete with the young by seeking to exceed the usual allotment of life's time and resources is selfish and futile–the

world follows the order of time itself and always moves forward.

- Death serves the goal of winnowing old thoughts by eliminating those who entertain them—older people assume that the era in which they lived their lives is normative for all other periods.
- Anger towards your children is a generational suicide.
- To seek to control assets and their utilization from beyond the grave is to ensure that the world will never progress beyond your level of expertise.
- To act like a God is the surest way to deprive yourself of salvation.
- Excessive greed means retaining more than is right for you.
- In reality, the spendthrift is a miser because he is the ultimate destination of the goods that have been squandered.
- The man who spends money to raise his social class or his ego is well along the road of destruction. Your only real legacy is that others think well of you after you have died because of the example that you have set.
- Often, those seeking to find dynasties seek to preserve their name rather than benefit their heirs.
- The average length of a generation is 25 to 30 years.
- After 100 years have passed or three generations, those who will receive your largess will only be related to you as follows: children 50%; grandchildren 25%; great-grandchildren 12.5%; great-great-grandchildren 6.25%; great-great-great grandchildren 3.1241%, that is five generations or 125 years. So, assuming that you live for 80 years, before another 80 years pass, your youngest direct relatives will only be related to you by about 3%. In the vast genetic shuffle, your card will come up about six times in 100 draws.

- You can forget the project of founding a dynasty and realize that your generosity should be confined to those who are alive to thank you for it.
- And by the way, think about transferring some wealth when your prospective heirs are still young enough to make a discernible difference in the quality of their lives and open doors of opportunity that would otherwise be closed to them.
- You cannot suppose that the future generation's areas of progress and human contribution or skillset is identical to yours.
- Above all else, you cannot use your success to belittle future generations or your money to control others.
- To leave some legacy is a mark of your contribution to the life process as a whole, but that legacy can take many forms other than only money.
- When you die, you will only keep the things you have given to others and nothing you have received in your lifetime.

Unfortunately, we often focus on the monetary value. But monetary value alone is an inadequate measure of real worth. Many of the most precious things in life cannot be purchased, and we can never scale them or directly convert them to a monetary unit. Leaving legacies of many types of creative achievements is likewise not scalable, but they are real for all of that.

My book's message is that we should strive to provide a monetary and non-monetary legacy for the coming two or three generations. Beyond this, with the possible exception of land, it is nearly impossible to calculate future values from present conditions. Few of today's most significant companies barely existed even twenty years ago, and many companies that were once household names now no longer exist. Money always changes form as it is invested in new assets to meet new needs. Capital exists to enable ideas. By leaving a monetary legacy to our immediate heirs, we are saving them from the exploitation and waste of resources that flow from poverty. Talent is stimulated by life challenges and is stifled by the artificial roadblock of poverty.

Our newspapers carry the daily record of those whose families are trapped in cycles of poverty, all of which are fed by having limited options. There are only 24 hours in a day and only seven days in a week. Genius does not keep a time-clock, of course. Still, if talent and the occasional intersection of opportunity with the means to take advantage of it means were constants, there would be no need to leave a legacy. All equal prosperity would be the ultimate chance of all people and all nations. Today, we know that equitable opportunity is not a reality. The exploitation of the weak and the unfortunate is our legacy from the beasts. What is human in us demands far more than to create more cunning human animals. We leave legacies so that civilization may proceed.

Only brutal minds respond first to force; the talented among us are motivated by desire and inspiration. Often mere chance, dishonesty, or cunning creates riches where little of lasting worth has been created. It is the privilege of those whose worth is primarily based on the net worth to support activities with higher social value. Naturally, the first is to see to those closest to us in blood and affinity. There is also a place for outreach to outsiders. A general benevolence should help us recall that the distinction between relatives and strangers breaks down beyond one or two generations. We are all part of the universal family of humankind. Those who do not see and respect the human dignity and freedom to grow without coercion of people near at hand will never learn to embrace a universal charity.

We live in exciting times. The baby boom generation has retired. The average life expectancy of both males and females is in the 80s in America. Meanwhile, the younger generation, the ones whose social security payments must support the extended retirement of the past generations, are coming to maturity. Younger generations are now growing up in a widespread dwindling post-war American middle-class. This new reality tends to breed mistrust and a lack of communication between generations.

We should think very clearly about the message we want to leave for our children. Suppose our only example to our children has been to set before them the example of conspicuous personal consumption. In that case, any legacy that we leave in money should come with the wish that they do not follow our example. Above all else, we will not imagine that it is wise for our heavy skeletal hand to reach from beyond the grave to constrain and limit them as they live their lives. Those whose experience of life has led them to conclude that their children should serve to enshrine their parent's memory are only retaining a vanity that should have been given up during their years of growth to maturity. Fully mature people realize that real wealth lies in the ability to share their wealth with future generations. Life is for the living; the ghosts of the past must finally let go. What is past must serve the future.

Before we can build trans-generational wealth, we need to create harmony between generations. We will never leave a legacy if we are unwilling to let go of what we have. It is not the business of the present generation to waste time building endless memorials to what has been but to prepare for future growth and development. The arrow of time flows in only one direction, and so must the resources of the earth.

CHAPTER 2

The Moral Grounds of Wealth

Vices make us blind; virtues make us see.

When we decide to generate generational wealth, we need a value system and skills to enhance our legacy.

Virtue, not wealth, is the goal of life. But wealth need not preclude virtue. What do I mean by this bold statement? My proposition is a simple one. Our pursuit of achieving wealth direct is rarely successful. Who does not wish to be wealthy? Yet so few are. The sheer desire for wealth leads many to undertake reckless behaviors or to look about for some never-failing guru who can turn a sow's ear into a silk purse by magic. By contrast, the great philosophers realized that what makes a person successful, shows in every action, and every endeavor. The pursuit of wealth that does not have the prerequisite character development usually ends in disaster. Either the expenditures will eat up savings before they can be usefully invested. Or savings will be poorly invested and thus yield meager returns. The book before you will try to address in a systemic manner the logical steps and practical techniques of wealth creation. However, creating wealth is of little use if it is only a personal goal. The wealth that does not survive a single generation can hardly be called wealth at all.

Wealth is, properly speaking, a means to ensure personal freedom. Wealth is a preventive measure to becoming co-opted by systems that will force us overtime to sell ourselves, our talents, and our time for less than we deserve. The proof of this modern trend is that in post-recession America absent wealth, one may be gradually forced to descend into the labor pool of relatively unsophisticated and unrewarding labor.

The modern dilemma is what this book will attempt to solve. I hope that I will show how to build lasting and straightforward wealth in a world where fundamental changes are now underway.

WEALTH GENERATES CULTURE

Wealth yields freedom. Freedom yields leisure (spare time). Spare time yields self-actualization and personal growth. Personal growth yields social contributions. And social contributions produce culture.

THE SUPPRESSION OF WEALTH

I have been privileged to experience the oppressive conditions that prevailed in Eastern Europe before the breakup of the Soviet Bloc. I have personally witnessed under what poor conditions people live, governed by communist regimes, which aimed to destroy people's religions and their values in the eastern states of Europe and Communist China. When I visited parts of my family in Eastern Germany before and after the wall came down in 1989, I saw run-down cities, gray and abandoned houses, and broken windows. I remember when I visited my aunt Berta in 1982 in Jena, a small town in communist Eastern Germany. She lived at that time in a typical multi-family house. Her bathrooms did not even have a flushing toilet. I could smell the distinct stench of cheap burned coal in every corner of the city. Later, in the nineties, I had met my cousin Jürgen in Eastern Germany when he was in his early thirties. He grew up in a country ruled by a communist government, and when he arrived in West Germany, his hunger for wealth was overwhelming.

Later in my life, when I immigrated to the United States in the late nineties, I saw a democracy where people are meant to be free and are guided by their strong moral values. They could trade and build wealth under the influence of this ethical conduct. However, since then, a lot has changed. I have witnessed that commercial advertisements and political power have undermined virtues. Today, it seems that we overly promote negative traits. Have you watched scenes on TV commercials where people envy their neighbors for having the latest products like a new car? Have you seen the ads that promote greed, lust, or other excessive behaviors? Vices seem to have become more acceptable in our lives today, even though we know that many of these negative character traits are not good for us. How can we keep our vices under control? Religions are one way to learn and teach basic morals. However, commonly accepted morals today have little to do with religion. Morals are the fundamental values for any wealthy society. They are known as the seven virtues, which are in contrast to the seven vices known as the seven deadly sins.

THE FORMULA FOR WEALTH

For the purposes of this book, let's agree to stick to the following seven virtues: *diligence, patience, kindness, humility, temperance, abstinence and gratitude.* Every one of us has the tendency to respect at least some of these virtues in one way or the other. But we are also often victims of our own *greed, lust, excess, pride, envy, wrath and sloth.*

I believe it is not hard to argue that a person who can balance the seven virtues and the seven vices will more likely succeed in life than someone obsessed with one or more of the seven *virtues* and *vices.* I picture the virtues and vices pinned on a steering wheel of a big old ship. When the ship follows a straight course on the ocean waters, the ship holds its course, and it will reach its destination. The upper part of the steering wheel is illustrated by the virtues. The lower part is filled with all the bad habits, the vices. Of course, the ship has to be maneuvered, so the steering wheel has to be turned. At some point, some vices will appear above the sea-line. They will appear on the surface. And some virtues will disappear under the sea-line. We live on earth, and sacrifices have to be made sometimes; in the end, it is not a perfect world. We all are prone to some of the vices at some point or the other.

Figure 2.1 The Wheel of Wealth™

So, I created The Wheel of Wealth™. For me, it is a compass that shows me the way to my integrity and, as I will describe later, ultimately to wealth. If I had known The Wheel of Wealth when I was younger, I would have done many things very differently. I would have had different friends, I would have seen their human weaknesses earlier, and I could have tried to guide them or look for other friends. I realize that many of my family members and friends have been and still are obsessed with all kinds of vices, but also virtues. I lost a close person years ago to the excessive overuse of alcohol and many other drugs. I lost another to his destructive political thoughts and activities related to obsessive national pride.

I have lost two others to their obsessive dedication to music. I have lost a very close friend to his addiction to extreme sports, and I have lost a very good early friend to excessive greed for financial success.

MY FRIENDS AND FAMILY

Luckily, the majority of my friends and family are excellent moral stewards. But I have lost my obsessed friends because their obsessions made them blind. I lost some of them because they have been behind bars for quite some time due to their bad habits. I have lost some friends because they lost their license to drive a car, or their right to travel internationally, so they could not visit me.

All of these friends are very poor today. Sure, some of them get by somehow. But many of them live from welfare and others. They have minimal access to financial resources, and their obsessions increasingly limit their world. I hardly talk to any of them anymore; in many cases, I got pulled into their negativity and obsessions very quickly, so I have started to avoid them altogether. I realize that our human weaknesses and strengths are the ones that guide us through our lives. They are like the directions on a compass. All of us are prone to all sorts of behaviors. And I realize that some of us tend to focus on habits that make us weaker while others focus on activities that make us stronger.

Furthermore, obsessions magnify certain human behaviors. Like a compass needle points to the North, people's passions point them in a specific direction. Every one of us has a personal North. It is the direction in which our destiny seems to push us towards. What's more, I believe, if the path is towards the human weaknesses, that person will become weaker and more impoverished. If the course is towards human strengths, he or she will become wealthier.

It appears to me like a secret formula for wealth. I have seen people who are kind, diligent, patient, humble, temperate, give rather than take and exercise abstinence become generally wealthier than people who live in lust, greed, excess, pride, envy, wrath, and sloth.

I have seen, with my own eyes, repeatedly how wealthy people have financial, human, and social capital, whereas poor people are economic and social liabilities. Of course, some wealthy people might be standoffish and even immoral. For example, some individuals today might believe that it was very shameless that John D. Rockefeller became so ultra-rich by selling these unbelievable amounts of crude oil to us, which are said to cause environmental issues today. And we indeed can find exceptions for completely immoral people who became rich and famous. I have also seen people who were angel-like individuals but never accumulated any wealth. However, I believe that people who can control their virtues and vices will become wealthier than individuals who can't.

ARE OUR GENERATIONS GETTING WEALTHIER?

Today, our contemporary society seems to make us more and more greedy. TV and social media ads show us how to increase our desire for one or another product. Companies want us to consume more than is good for us, to make us overly prideful for what we can buy or own, and to make us covet our neighbor's possessions. These character traits combined tend to loosen the control of our temper and make us downright lazier. I will go so far as to say that watching too many ads will make us inevitably more miserable. Of course, all commercial ads are made to promote products created by people who want to make money. Commercials are generally not designed to make the people who watch the commercials richer. There is nothing wrong with that. Except, if you wish to become wealthy, just ceasing to watch ads will not help. So, what will help?

When the code of interpersonal behavior, which is considered right or acceptable in a particular society, is suppressed or even destroyed, that society will, sooner or later, end up in poverty. There are many recent examples of countries that drowned in corruption while their citizens became dirt-poor.

Recently, I watched a show entitled *"Is Greed Good?"* on Fox News for Business. I was shocked by the arguments of the participants. Everybody seemed to assume that greed could be a part of regular business practice to make money instead of asking at what point greed will destroy a business. I believe greed is only in the way of getting wealthy. Greed is an intense and selfish desire for individual wealth. But building generational wealth has other motives–motives like virtues, kindness, and charity. To maximize generational wealth, individuals must minimize greed.

My conclusion is that people must learn and grow up with strong morals if they want to become wealthy. It is clear to me that people need a solid moral foundation to prosper. I believe when people's morals are suppressed, they will tend to become poor. Morals are the basis for wealth. Morals lay the ground for our education and all our actions. Without morals, education is just manipulation, so activism without moral grounds will ultimately lead to poverty and tyranny. When people lose their morals, they will slide into poverty.

To build wealth for generations, we first need to teach our children morals.

IS BEING POOR IS A STATE OF MIND?

Entrepreneur and investor Robert Kiyosaki says: *"broke is when you run out of money, poor is a state of mind."* Here is how my seven-year-old son responded to this statement. I asked him if he thinks that a rich man is poor when he loses all his money. Instantly, he replied "no, he will do the same things he did when he got rich, and then he will have all his money back."

His answer to me was remarkable because he replied so quickly and because his response triggered an exciting thought in me that has kept me busy. My son instinctively implied that being rich is not about having money; he said being rich means knowing how to make money. Later that day, I asked myself if a poor man would be considered rich when he suddenly owns millions of dollars. The answer must also be: "no, because he will do the same things he did when he got poor, and then he will have no money again."

WEALTH IS A MATTER OF HABITS

So, my conclusion is that becoming wealthy must be a matter of education and habits. Many generations have worked hard to become wealthy, but only a few were able to do so. During my research on this subject, I discovered a master plan behind why so many people do not become wealthy: our society teaches too few of us to become wealthy. In this book, we will see why this has been so for so many generations. Today, each generation tries to create its very own form of wealth. Almost everybody in each generation except a tiny number of elite individuals has failed miserably in all generations. Do you know any family, which can live exclusively from the returns of their financial assets?

GENERATIONS OF WEALTH

Over the last 150 years, The Missionary Generation (1860-1882), The Lost Generation (1883-1900), The Greatest Generation (1901-1924), The Silent Generation (1925-1942), The Baby Boomers (1943-1960), Generation X (1961-1980), and The Millennials are known as Generation Y and Internet Generation (1981-2000) have each had their challenges and hopes. Individuals of Generation Z, the people born after the year 2000, are in college-age now. They will be the first generation with a significant advantage: due to the never-seen ease of access to knowledge and tools, the new generations, Generation Z, has the potential to finally break through the paradigm that keeps us from creating financial assets for generations.

In this book, I will try to explain how to build practical wealth for generations. It will show us why we need to get out of our comfort zones and create wealth. We will be encouraged to rethink our entire past and future career and re-evaluate our financial habits. The book will show us through practical examples of why it is essential to create financial products in our lives instead of only buying financial products. This book will tell us how exactly we can do that. I have gone through nearly all of the scenarios described in this book. I envision it as a complete guide to converting our lives from average, credit burdened individuals to team-building, sophisticated, influential investors who can create wealth for generations.

FAMILY VALUES

With all the knowledge and habits but no concept for family values, we cannot build generational wealth.

Mormon families, for example, strive to continue to exist as families after earthly death; and they live with the expectation that they will live again with their ancestors and their eventual descendants. This is why family values are the cornerstone of Mormon families. Roles, responsibilities, and behavioral expectations are taught in every detail.

THE WEALTH OF NATIONS VS GENERATIONS

On March 9, 1776, Adam Smith published his book *The Wealth of Nations*. In the 18th century, the idea of nations was forming rapidly. In Europe, people were more loyal to their religions than their nations before the dawn of the 18th century. Wikipedia writes, *"With the emergence of a national public sphere and an integrated, country-wide economy in 18th Century England, people began to identify with the country at large, rather than the smaller unit of their family, town or province. The early emergence of a popular patriotic nationalism took place in the mid-18th century and was actively promoted by the government and by the writers and intellectuals of the time"*. These developments were predominant, of course as well in the new world America. The 18th-century American mastermind Adam Smith must have been a trendy fellow when he wrote his book *The Wealth of Nations*. He published it just four months before the United States Declaration of Independence was signed, which is known as the day of the American Nation's birth.

His concepts on the *Division of Labor, Money, and Debt* helped tremendously set the course for the development of our current economic system that has made many nations very rich. The basic idea of the *Division of Labor* is that individuals specialize in their work skills, learn a trade, and earn money by selling these skills to employers or their customers. This arrangement turned out to be an ultra-effective way for nations to become very wealthy. The most recent example is China. Many people have been added to the Chinese economic system as employees over the last twenty years. As reported by many sources, in 2012, China became the second wealthiest nation on earth. But two significant developments happened at the same time when China grew more prosperous as a nation: a tremendous number of people started their businesses. It became very wealthy as well, whereas an even higher number of people and families became "fang nu" (房奴), who are housing slaves as they are often called in China. Based on a February 20, 2013, Bloomberg report, the number of *housing slaves* in China grew out of proportion. Bloomberg reports that "*many Chinese people will need a lifetime to pay off their mortgages; some pay more than seventy percent of their salaries to service their mortgages. It seems, even in China, with a culture of more than 5,000 years old with a long tradition of economic activities, has not learned or forgotten how to transfer wealth from generation to generation successfully*". A Chinese saying is: "Fu bu guo san dai" (富不过三代), which means that wealth does not pass three generations.

It is an absolute rarity that the wealth of a family lasts for three generations. The first generation works extremely hard so that the second generation reaps the benefits and may see the value of hard work. But the third generation has forgotten all about it. By the time the fourth generation arrives, the wealth is squandered.

So, I ask, is it possible to transfer and even grow wealth throughout more than three generations? Many factors prevent wealth from effectively being transferred, such as estate taxes, legal costs of probate, and excess consumption of surpluses before it can be invested. Therefore, it is crucial to instill a detailed understanding of social and financial capital into the next generation's daily life. There is a tendency for successful entrepreneurs to mistrust the sharing of responsibility and discretion over hard-earned assets. And this often results in an attitude that says in effect, "I made it on my own, why can't you do the same." Of course, the fallacy of this logic is that time, and circumstances change. An example that will come readily to mind is the generational difference between young men leaving the armed forces in the post-WW II period when extensive GI benefits paid for a college education. In contrast, today's veterans' level of benefits mostly won't allow such investment.

A further factor is a difference in temperament and talent between persons within families. Not all skills are of a business nature. Where would the world be without its artists, musicians, and skilled artisans?

This book's essential purpose is to provide a source of information and inspiration to build and retain the wealth between generations. In contrast to Adam Smith's book, this book describes how individuals, families, and whole generations can build and maintain wealth through entrepreneurship and sophisticated investments. Small groups of people like families and larger groups like communities are the foundation for all nations' wealth. Since the dawn of the modern economy, however, nations' wealth has been the economy's driving force. It is about time that individuals, their families, and whole generations form a similar manifesto of economic progress. Only a fraction of families became wealthy over the past centuries, and all other families have to start building their financial foundation from scratch with each new generation. It is now time to give young generations a tool so that they can build wealth for generations. Even Adam Smith hinted in his work at the limits of labor division and the wealth of nations. He wrote that workers who are too specialized could develop "*mental mutilation*," which could negatively impact a nation's wealth.

It is time to think about how we can make families and whole generations wealthy. Today, almost everyone relies almost entirely on one or more salaries per household. When the salary fails to come in, most people start to struggle, begin to panic, and like drug addicts, they run for the next available job to satisfy their creditors. It does not have to be that way. Our forefathers and -mothers worked hard to create the knowledge, wisdom, and tools that we can use today to live a more satisfying life. I will demonstrate how to use this knowledge and the tools that free us from financial dependencies, personal time limitations, and constant concerns about our job security and social status.

WHY DID I WRITE A BOOK LIKE THIS?

After working for many years as a business consultant, advising large companies leveraging emerging business technologies, I have learned a lot about how businesses work. I have also seen how many failed and why they failed. I saw employees crawling to their job sites every morning, not always trying to hide their personal, often financial, problems while producing rather mediocre results. In the last few years before I started my own companies, I sometimes even found myself among them in the same state of mind.

What changed my view of the financial world and my entire career was converting my hard-earned retirement money account into a self-directed retirement account, which freed up financial assets that I had to manage. With my savings and some additional financial assets that were available to me, I was now in charge of several financial assets in several different types of asset classes.

Over the years, I have made many investment mistakes, but I have had several successes, which now provide my family with some passive income. Instead of worrying about finding my next job, I worry now about how to invest our assets to provide us with passive income. Our passive income is currently only a fraction of what I have received as a salary in the past. But my family and I now have much more free time, and we have adopted habits like *fiscal fasting* or *spending detoxification*, as some people call controlling their finances.

We have to learn how to be smart investors instead of learning to be intelligent employees. Luckily, I started small years ago when I worked as an employee, preparing for my new job as a sophisticated investor.

My task then was to take that little seed of wealth and turn it into something bigger. Something that my family can pass on to our future generations. In my book, I invite you to follow me on my journey.

BUILDING WEALTH WITHOUT GREED OR FEAR

I believe that fear kills more dreams than failure ever will. I know that, as Mark Twain concluded, courage is not the absence of fear; it is control of the same. I have experienced that greed and fear have prevented me from being financially free. I remember when I invested a large sum of our family money in precious metal. I often woke up at night to check on gold and silver prices to confirm that my fundamental assumptions for being in precious metals were still right. So, I learned over time to control my greed and my fears. This book demonstrates how we can build a kingdom of wealth without extreme desire and anxiety; it shows how to reduce financial risk over time. I wrote this book for people who want to build sophisticated wealth over generations.

NECESSARY ENDINGS

When you read this book, you might realize, as I did along my journey, that we must forget things versus learning new things. We will see that it is essential for our families and us to put an end to bad habits. We will realize that we should focus on practices that increase our wealth. This book will help us identify our bad financial habits, and it will show us how we can put an end to some of our bad habits so that we can focus on the practices we benefit from.

Albert Einstein once said: *"Insanity is doing the same thing over and over again and expecting different results."* Quitting bad habits and parting from some bad assets in our portfolio will free us, so we have more time to try out different passions, things that bring out our portfolio's full potential. Much like a gardener prunes the branches of a tree so that they can produce more fruit, we will learn how to manage our financial assets so that dead assets will disappear from our portfolio and good assets become more reliable and stable. We will discover that many of our most valuable assets might not even be financial. We might notice our current financial assets held in our bank, and our retirement accounts might not be the right assets for us if we want to reach our personal goals. We do not have to manage our investments in detail, but we have to evaluate them overtime or lose them sooner or later. Some of our assets may be our skills. But we need to consider, like a gardener its plants, which ones to keep because they make us more prosperous and replace them because they hold us back. I am inviting you to read this book to leave the financial la-la-land and go with me on an exciting journey.

PRIDE AND ENVY

Out of the seven vices, envy and pride are, in my opinion, the most threatening habits when it comes to building wealth. And envy is much worse than greed since an envious person is not only rendered unhappy by his envy, but that person also wishes to inflict misfortune on others, which will most likely spoil many valuable personal and business relationships.

Some see pride as the worst vice there is; they say pride makes us blind. I often like to use the words ignorance and arrogance when I attempt to explain what pride is. Excessive pride tends to make us lose focus on facts and neglect the needs of our fellow citizens.

Whether the world is heading for a prolonged economic emergency like James Howard Kunstler describes in his book entitled *The Long Emergency,* or towards a robust economic period of growth, I recommend that you evaluate your emotions related to pride and envy. Whether the world economy is running on extremely cheap crude oil, like it did in the 1990s and late 2010s, or whether the world is fueled by unfordable expensive energy, I decided that I want to be a responsible and robust member of my community. I don't want to be a financial burden to my friends and family, and I don't want to be overly proud of what I have and what I am.

DILIGENCE AND PATIENCE

I wrote this book to share some of my most essential insights in finance that are as unique as they are controversial, but also practical and straightforward. The book skips complicated financial lingo to increase readability for a broader public. I have gained insights during my career as a business analyst, business manager, board member, business owner, mentor, project manager, and investor.

People tend to rely on the government and institutions to fix problems. Trapped in ever-increasing time commitments to their employers and financial creditors, people seem to forget how to cook fresh food, parent their kids, maintain their marriages, or manage their financial assets. Contrary, during the COVID-19 health crisis of 2020, this changed for a short period. Suddenly, yeast, flour, and baking goods were sold out in stores because stay-at-home orders gave people finally more time away from their employers, which led to an unseen spike in demand for these goods.

However, it became also clear that many families in the United States live paycheck to paycheck. When the breadwinners of these households lost their jobs, most of their families would be living on the streets within a few months without government help. If they don't find a job, they will likely depend on welfare and are dependent on people who were prepared financially and mentally. It is your choice to be among one group or the other.

You might ask yourself, how can so many families live paycheck to paycheck? In my opinion, it has all to do with uncontrolled emotions like lacking diligence and patience. It also has to do with financial education and the things they buy.

Many people believe that they act like investors when instead, they are only consumers. Today, average investors buy financial products. In contrast, sophisticated investors buy assets and sell financial products. Almost all ordinary investors today invest by purchasing financial products that sophisticated investors have created. And most average investors do not know the difference between financial products and financial assets. Average investors who buy financial products focus exclusively on capital gains. Sophisticated investors purchase financial products to create value. Even though professional traders got pretty good at trading nowadays, they are not buying assets for income; they exclusively bet their investments would gain in value. In part II, I will explain how sophisticated investors develop their assets.

Short-term traders are speculators who buy and sell assets in a short period, make a profit, and move on. Long-term traders tend to regularly transfer money into a securities account with the hope of receiving a better return than from a savings account. Almost all investment management companies who manage retirement plans today operate on this principle. While trading is an excellent way to make money, traders miss a crucial opportunity in modern capitalism: creating value. Traders hope that their investment value will increase but have no way to add value to the investment. This lack of control is why, in my opinion, traders are not sophisticated investors. Traders have a job. They are not sophisticated investors.

There is one other dimension that is crucial for every investor: asset income. I have very successful friends who won't buy a larger asset if it doesn't produce any significant steady income from day one. If they have to put money down every month to keep the asset, they will not buy it. Their philosophy is: "if an asset does not produce income, I don't buy it."

I wrote this book for anyone who wants to become someone who invests in financial assets instead of just buying financial products. If you care about your family and you are willing to make drastic changes in your life, if you feel the urge to build a robust and very unconventional asset portfolio for generations to come, then this book is for you. You will learn how to manage your assets in two dimensions. It is like driving a car on the autobahn with no speed limit. You control two dimensions: direction and speed. You do not want to be too fast or will end up in the ditch after the next curve. If you invest, you control two dimensions: asset income and asset value. Both are equally important to reach your target destination. If you mismanage one, you will end up either in the ditch or in the wrong place.

GRATITUDE

You want to be a two-dimensional investor and appreciate and manage the income stream (portfolio income) and the capital gains at the same time, even if they are small. No asset can be a perfect investment unless you recognize and manage both. Warren Buffet sums it up to *"Never lose!"* His approach does not mean someone else has to lose when you win. The best deals are always win-win deals. I wrote this book for people who want to learn more about two-dimensional wealth management. The goal of this book is to provide an alternative and, in my opinion, a far more dependable and future-oriented approach than standard practices offered by most investment advisors, banks, and wealth management firms. This book will show the reader how to appreciate every asset from its core step-by-step and increase wealth over time.

HUMILITY

Early in my life, I pursued a career in economic informatics, business analysis, and project management as a business consultant. For almost 20 years, I worked for fortune 500 companies and numerous start-ups in management and consultancy. I have worked in Munich, Frankfurt, Stuttgart, Paris, London, Tokyo, Monterey, Mexico, Singapore, and in many cities in the United States.

Something happened to me. I realized that my career goals were counterproductive to what I wanted to achieve in my life. I have had great successes as a business analyst, consultant, and manager in many fields and industries for almost twenty years. But with each promotion, I only got more work, and my assignments got riskier and more time-consuming, whereas my salary only grew moderately. In 2008, the inevitable change happened when I realized that I needed to change how I earn money. I stopped working in my good paying job and took one year off. I could not wait to down-shift and re-arrange my life.

First, I looked at all my financial and personal assets in great detail and decided to make sure they were all in order. I sold what did not produce any or enough income, and I restructured or paid off the debt that was attached to some of my assets. It was the most significant inventory of my entire life.

I also felt a little bit like John Galt, a fictional character in the novel *Atlas Shrugged*. John Galt seemed to have disappeared one day for no apparent reason. I, too: I retracted from the typical business-as-usual life to take care of my family matters, including our financial future. I am writing this book to express my thoughts and experience, which I made while learning to speak the language of someone who does not get paid for the work they do but for the financial results they produce. Investors get paid for results and not for their time spent on a job or the work performed.

I welcome you to learn to speak a–straightforward–financial language of a small group of people who control a disproportionate amount of wealth and political power in the world today. I even urge you to learn that language and become more literate in financial matters for your good and our children. Your financial independence and literacy will increase the chance that your family, neighborhood, and city are afloat even in an economic crisis. Emerging technology is readily available and makes it easier than ever to become a steward of your financial future. Start small, get financially educated, get out of your comfort zone, and get out of the rat race!

ARE YOU READY?

When the automobile powered by a combustion engine became popular in the 19th century, not everyone felt comfortable or even capable of controlling a machine propelled by explosive fuel. So, I understand when you think you are not ready to grab that steering wheel and press that pedal of your brand new, environmentally friendly, trendy, and super fast vehicle of the Twenty-first Century called a sophisticated investor. But if you dare, take a seat and read on!

CHAPTER 3

The 3 M's: Morals, Mind and Money

"Being broke is when you run out of money,
and being poor is a state of mind."

—Robert Kiyosaki, Bestselling Author, Entrepreneur

I hope that my book will help you become a sophisticated investor. But, as I wrote this book, I found myself wondering: what are the critical elements of being a sophisticated investor. I came up with three terms: morals, mind, and money.

If a poor person, without the possession of morals, had sudden financial success, that person would likely ultimately become impoverished again within a short time. Similarly, long-lasting business success depends also upon certain qualities of mind, such as thinking critically, evaluating various assets using imagination and foresight, motivating people, leadership skills, and, above all, the ability to appreciate opportunities when one encounters them. Lastly, I realized that some financial backing is essential to become wealthy, even with all the world's morals and minds.

I would say that building generational wealth is the process of building a foundation of generational morals, a cultivated mind, and the ability to accumulate money for investing. Building a foundation of money is the most visible and instantly usable part of wealth. However, in my experience, most people today would not expect that refining their morals and developing their minds are assets that are prerequisites for creating money. Morals are required because, ultimately, no society could survive if people mostly achieve wealth through cheating and immoral behavior. Furthermore, a financially educated mind is also needed to build assets and create real value.

With every increase in one of these three elements, morals, mind, and money, each succeeding generation develops their financial and social wealth.

In 2013, I asked an artist to illustrate the concept of morals, mind, and money in a picture. Under my instructions, he drew a typical image of a lever, which can be used to lift a rock from the ground. The longer the bar is, the easier it is to push the lever down to lift the stone. The saying *"to move mountains"* literally has to do with the principle of leverage.

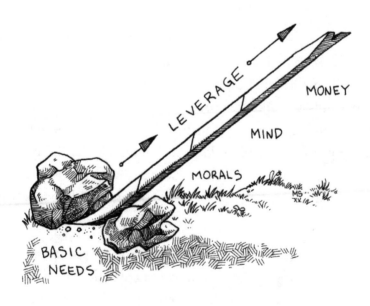

Figure 2.2 Morals, Minds and Money create Wealth through Leverage (illustration by Matt Smith, copyright 2020 Ingemar Anderson)

What is now apparent is that if someone or something tries to take authority over your morals, mind, or money, they will impact your wealth. In communist regimes, religions have been suppressed, which led to the decline of both national and private wealth. In all societies, the mind is under constant influence from sources like the media, the educational system, and public opinion. My advice is: if you would like to build a family legacy and create generational wealth, you should find and live out of your very own validated system of morals and develop a concept for your education.

CHAPTER 4

Are You a Wealth Creator?

"There is a time when panic is the appropriate response."

—Eugene Kleiner (1923–2003)

On November 26, 1973, President Richard Nixon proposed a nationwide 50 mph speed limit for passenger vehicles and a 55 mph speed limit for trucks and buses. It was an emergency response to the 1973 oil crisis. He imposed the speed limit because of a crisis: the first worldwide oil shock. Gas was limited, and so was the speed for cars and trucks on the highway.

Our financial sophistication is no different. If our financial sophistication is limited, our financial possibilities are limited, too. We live in a crisis-mode. But if we overcome our financial crises, our options will be unlimited. Today, in some countries, there are no speed limits on highways between larger cities. You can go as fast as you wish; your judgment only limits you.

Thinking without limits is how we must act as a citizen in the Twenty-first Century. As long as our ideas are legal and ethical, we shouldn't feel limited. We want to switch to the highest gear possible if we need to.

Too many people don't use higher gears in their financial activities. Instead, they are crawling along in a traffic jam, sometimes even idling in neutral, stuck with thousands of other people all trying to move forward. But they are losing the game. Without shifting into second or higher gear, they will never pick up any speed.

When we feel like we are one of these slow drivers, we will need to first invest in our financial education. We need to find out how good our financial knowledge and experience is. This chapter will support us in defining this baseline.

We all come from different backgrounds, have different levels of education and different experiences. So, the starting point for every individual reader is unique. During the late nineties, when crude oil was relatively cheap, we could all experience a decade of the financial boom. In contrast, the first decade of the twenty-first century was economically challenging. Depending on what we expect during the coming decade, our investment ideas might vary. However, this book will show us that the primary financial rules apply during all economic periods and situations.

Every person has a different background in life, and everybody carries different baggage. Some might have had a difficult childhood growing up in poverty. Some might have lived in abundance their whole life, and some might lack financial education in some areas or some bad financial habits, or some might not be interested in the topic of increasing their wealth. It matters where a person is coming from when it comes to financial education. I wrote this book to make financial literacy more accessible and fun for everybody, and to raise the level of urgency for financial education.

Now, let's first find out how we organize our personal situation. Are we rushing from one task to another? Are we employed, and is our job taking too many hours? Do we see our children at best shortly before they go to bed? Are our vacations typically no longer than two weeks? Are we getting nowhere with our financial plan? We do not own a business, and we do not own real estate? If we answered yes to at least one question, we should think about improving our financial sophistication. Read this chapter thoroughly to find out what we can do to improve our chances of becoming a more sophisticated investor. We will start identifying our own financial and personal assets and start managing them.

Taking these first steps might be very challenging for many people. Most people are addicted to their habits. Becoming a sophisticated investor does not mean to give up the person we are. But it means to get in control of our habits.

We might be addicted to our powerlessness and victim-hood, or we might be overly attached to our sense of entitlement. Before we can gain control over our financial situation, we need to find out what kind of person we are and get in control of our habits. For example, if we collect all sorts of coupons to save money when we go shopping, we might focus too much on our expenses instead of becoming a smarter investor.

THE AVERAGE INVESTOR

I claim that the average investor today is nothing else than a consumer. They buy financial products, which sophisticated investors have created. Many attributes describe the average investor: he or she is an employee who pays a mortgage or rent, and almost all income comes from one or more salaries, whereas most of the income goes to daily expenses. None of their income is passive income. Today, the vast majority of the western population can be categorized as average investors.

THE SOPHISTICATED INVESTOR

First off, being a sophisticated investor has nothing to do with a job. It is a lifestyle. The typical definition of a sophisticated investor is a person who is considered to have sufficient investing experience and knowledge to weigh the risks and merits of an investment opportunity. Today, many businesses and organizations expect a certain net worth and income before a person can be classified as a sophisticated or accredited investor. Such an investor is eligible to buy into certain investment opportunities, such as pre-IPO securities, that are considered "non-disclosure" or "non-prospectus" issues. Typically, this type of investor must have either a net worth of $2.5 million or have earned more than $250,000 for the past two years to qualify.

But these requirements can only be met as a result of a certain life style. More important is how sophisticated investors became sophisticated in the first place.

They follow a simple but effective formula:

$$P = I + D + E + A$$

The financial product P is the result of activities related to:

(I)	Innovation
(D)	Development
(E)	Execution
(A)	Acceleration (Marketing, Sales and Operation)

Sophisticated investors create financial products. The entire right side of the formula describes the work of the sophisticated investor. Just by successfully following this formula, a person will become a sophisticated investor.

The left side of the formula (P) is for the average investor, which I call the consumer. The right side of the formula is for the sophisticated investor.

When average investors say they invest, they typically buy financial products. Today, most people assume that both sides of the equation represent investment activities. However, purchasing financial products and selling financial products are two completely different activities. The actions of average investors are limited to buying financial products. Sophisticated investors design financial products. They generate business blueprints. In this book, we will only learn more about the right side of the equation. We will read how we can make financial products. We will not learn about how to buy financial products. Although buying financial products is an essential part of our economy, we need to know that financial products typically only make the people wealthy who created them.

I+D+E+A activities of sophisticated investors are very similar to the activities of entrepreneurs. Both the investor and the entrepreneur invent, develop, implement, market, and sell products. The only difference is that the investor operates on a more abstract, passive level. The investor has a business focus, whereas the entrepreneur typically focuses on the product and the company itself. While the entrepreneur creates products and services directly and is also more involved in running the company, the investor has a more passive role in every activity. However, the investor executes far greater control over the entire business and can hire and fire the company's CEO. Entrepreneurs are, therefore, also called active investors, and investors are often called passive investors.

An employee generally picks one profession. An employee is, for example, a scientist or researcher, a developer or project manager, a marketing person, or a salesperson. Like most people, investors also have one field they are passionate about, but they need to understand more than one profession. They will need to work with scientists, other inventors, developers, project managers, and salespeople. Investors also need to be fundraisers and good masters of funds. Of course, investors always work with a team of people, so they typically need to possess high social capital, which allows them to interact intelligently with all other specialists.

WHAT ARE FINANCIAL PRODUCTS?

Financial products are investment vehicles that are made by sophisticated investors. These are investment funds, government or other bonds, insurance policies, futures, options, swaps, cash deposits (CD's), and simple products like our currency or complex products like collateralized debt obligations (CDO's). All intangible assets are financial products, which also include intellectual property and other rights. But if we take it further, a rental property that produces cash flow is also a financial product even though it is a tangible product. For example, if an investor buys a run-down property, remodels it as a special needs home, and rents it out to a company that runs senior homes, the investor created a financial product. The senior home company uses the rental to run their business to make money.

When we sell and establish a financial product in the market, we can be considered a sophisticated investor based on my book. The product will make us richer while focusing on our team that brings to life more financial products. Hence, it pays off to be a sophisticated investor in many ways. Sophisticated investors are the dream clients of most financial services firms, as they generate much more money when working with them than with average investors. For example, J.P. Morgan Chase Bank gives some of its customers Chase Private Client (CPC) Accounts. They receive many perks around the bank's services, like free international money wiring, safe deposit boxes, etc.

Typically, people have certain expectations about sophisticated investors: they can hold their investments indefinitely (the funds do not need to be liquidated for cash needs). They can assume a total loss of investment principal without causing severe damage to their overall net worth.

Investor	Type	Activities	Income	Taxes & Benefits
Average	Employee	Buy financial products	Earned	High taxes, close to no benefits
Active	Business owner	Create, operate financial products	Passive	Little taxes, some benefits
Passive	Accredited, sophisticated	Create and control financial products	Passive	Close to no taxes, determines all terms

Figure 4.1 Comparison Average, Active and Passive Investors.

The table shows where the average, active and passive investors receive their income from earned income from a job, while passive income comes from financial assets that produce income for the investor.

Average investors will benefit the most from reading this book. This book will still be valuable as a convenient source of information about many aspects of assets and asset management for active and passive investors.

Wherever you are in your life now, the goal of this book is to make you and your family wealthier and increase your financial sophistication.

CHAPTER 5

No money needed!

The wealthy can create something from nothing while average people have to pay for everything.

Being financially sophisticated is the fundamental requirement for being financially free. When people roll up their sleeves, start a business, and create something of value, financial wealth and freedom should be expected to follow.

But today, too many times, financially sophisticated people seem to be mistrusted, assumed to be liars, cheaters, and often even immoral. I am sure you remember at least one of the latest financial scandals of people who have mishandled large sums of public money, created pyramid schemes, or received unjustifiably high amounts of money in bonuses and salaries. In such an environment, it seems easy to argue against an urgent need for more financially sophisticated people.

To achieve financial sophistication, we will need to re-learn certain simple economic principles. We will need to start spending our money and time in a way so that we lay the groundwork for our children and grandchildren to live the dream that we all aspire to–it is the dream of personal financial freedom. It is a journey of generations that our fathers and mothers have started. Today, the level of uncertainty in both goals and the means to achieve them is undermined by systematic uncertainty. This uncertainty has many sources:

political upheaval, distance from centers of power and of economic concentration by the mass of our citizens, and an increasingly competitive world global climate, and the general speeding-up of events.

Many people are waking up, though, with the nightmare of private and public financial disasters that have been all around us in recent years. Our current financial habits have already pushed many people into financial ruin because of the assumption of overwhelming debt burdens. Yet we still tend to worship the gross domestic product. Even at the national level, we tend to forget that the GDP is not a sure-fire gauge of economic health. America's GDP is primarily a reflection of private domestic consumption, and it does not tell us anything about whether it has been generated by capital or by labor. How can the use of resources alone be a gauge of productivity? The critical point is that private consumption accounts for more than 2/3 of the entire GDP in a service economy and is rising every year. Where then is innovation occurring? America still leads in new product development, but we should not forget that these innovations' profits may be unrecoverable for the average consumer. These conditions show how necessary underlying financial sophistication is. In an economy, we cannot presume simple cause and effect chains. Instead, it becomes challenging to trace the effects of, for example, financial stimulus packages. The old concept of Keynesian Economics was that fiscal stimulus had a direct and immediate impact on the economy's health. A moment's reflection though it will show that in a world economy, the incentive of consumer spending in a consumer-oriented nation may increase wealth mostly in those countries farther down the national economic pyramid. At present, the textile industry is dominated by offshore exporters to purchase new clothing then is really to send dollars over-seas rather than to strengthen our national declining union textile factories. Even such an action as drinking more coffee may impoverish the soil and the general wealth fare of coffee exporting nations. How is this so? If we buy coffee at what we now call fair-trade prices only, the export of coffee causes the domestic population that harvests the coffee beans to fall deeper into servitude to large coffee plantations. So, we describe the dynamic of victimization in the modern world, and it takes sophistication not to fall victim to changing economic conditions.

I wrote this book for the average person to help improve his or her financial situation. This book discusses income and asset value control and explores the means that may be employed to control our own emotions when triggered by greed, lust, excess, pride, envy, wrath, and sloth. In the short-term, this might lead to some sacrifices that people will have to make.

For example, I have tried to teach my son the virtue of patience by showing him the benefits of deferred consumption: I offered him one candy now or two candies after dinner. Financially sophisticated people understand this concept of patience and deferred gratification very well because they are essential prerequisites for investing. They know how to wait to make money. The average person likes instant gratification, and the current overall economy prefers that too. Instant gratification might support the GDP in the short-run. However, it will tend to lower the total national resource base in the long-run because the money spent in consumption will no longer be available for personal or entrepreneurial investment.

Certain people might not like this book since overall consumption and economic growth might stagnate in the short term when more people follow my advice. But more people will become financially free by following the prescriptions in this book than would occur if they proceeded with mindless consumption while awaiting a winning lottery ticket.

As we become more financially sophisticated, self-reliant, and trusting in our talents and resources, the offer of a corporate job will become less attractive. Instead, we may wish to pursue our sense of personal mission by utilizing our talents and investigating the many opportunities available in our immediate environment.

In a world of financially educated, independent, and entrepreneurial employees, the old personnel management method becomes both unnecessary and counterproductive because self-starters supervision is often more a hindrance than a help. Where then will corporations find the automatons that formerly constituted the majority of their workforce? The answer has been by exporting low-level employment to third world nations. Domestically, eco-friendly campuses characterize the most creative companies where management prizes ideas and communication over routine fear-based compliance with corporate mandates.

When we treat employees as children who are only looking for an opportunity to misbehave, these employees tend to adopt the same behaviors that we try to prevent by supervising them like children. In such a working environment, habits like confidence and self-reliance, which are personality prerequisites for independent investing, are stifled daily by working in such a job. How can this vicious cycle of demoralization be broken? Many employees I know use their leisure time after work for nothing other than merely restoring their confidence and energy level to face the same dull routine on the following day. On the flip side, when people become financially more independent, the pool of skilled and talented employees will shrink dramatically. How can companies still get the work done and compete in the world economy?

The answer Artificial Intelligence. With AI-supported automation, corporations don't need to rely on a human workforce and salaried positions.

Many of my friends, for instance, run small businesses. Some got into financial trouble after 9/11 and the crisis of 2008 and had to reduce their workforce. These employers shared with me their experience when they had to tell some of their long-time employees that they would have to lay them off. These employees had previously depended upon their employer to support them and their families over many years. It was a devastating situation for both the employee and the employer. It was painful for the employer because he could no longer support them financially. And it was difficult for the employees because their boss, whom they had looked up to as a source of stability and strength, had to admit his limitations in the declining economy.

How much less painful it would have been if the employer had known that his employees could depend upon a reliable personal safety net provided by their financial investments to serve as a source of income? The nature of that safeguard will vary with the investment levels and the type of assets that can provide income during times of reduced income from labor. In the fast-approaching era of artificial intelligence, relying on income from work and government support alone is becoming increasingly risky. It is one of the primary motivations for me to write this book to prevent that sense of desperation in people who follow such a predictable path in their careers. In a world of skilled labor performed by humans, lay-offs are not the exception; they are the rule.

When the concepts in my book became widely accepted, more people would experience personal freedom and security, lessen the financial fear that has governed so many of us. When employees are treated as individuals rather than merely fungible labor or mere production capacity, humanity might finally rise to the next level. It becomes clear that companies that adopt such a new human-centered economy combined with deploying artificial intelligence will have a better chance of prosperity.

To obtain this degree of security and freedom, employees will have to change their habits and become more financially responsible. They will have to make sacrifices in their lives by delaying consumption to have starter capital to invest. Dave Ramsey says in his book *The Total Money Makeover*, "*a proven plan for financial fitness would take into consideration the following advice: ...stop buying with money you do not have things you don't need to impress people you don't like*".

I challenge you to rethink the way you have traditionally made money. You can only contribute to a positive future for your children when you are first really free yourself. Financial freedom then is both a spiritual and a material quest.

To understand how limited your present freedom is, you might consider the following graph. Have a look at the typical income distribution of the working class, middle class, and the class called "The 1%".

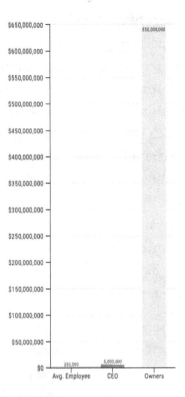

Figure 5.1 Report in "Income and Income Discrepancies" between average employees, the CEO and the owner of BMW. These numbers were presented by Helmut Creutz in www.humane-wirtschaft.de

The average employee at BMW AG, including management at BMW AG, made 200,000 euro in 2011. Robert Reithofer, CEO of BMW, made about 6 million euros in 2011. The owning family of BMW received about 650 million euros.

Of course, there is nothing wrong with the fact that company owners make a lot of money. Creating and owning valuable assets like BMW AG is what I propose in this book, and the fact that families and individuals have done it demonstrates that creating and owning such assets is possible and very effective. In the graphic above, we can hardly see the income of an average employee and manager of a company like BMW AG. Compared to the owner's profit, we can barely even see the salary of the CEO, although some people might even criticize him for pocketing too much money. The current company owners, however, received 650 million euros through dividends in 2011 by having an armada of employees work for mere nothing spending most of their time offering mostly nothing else than their skilled labor. How much difference would it make to most people's quality of life if the shares of income are equal and more equitable? Equitability and equality, at least historically speaking, have never been attainable except forcefully in the case of totalitarian societies like National Socialism in Germany or Communism. The better course towards a redistribution of societal resources is to take not the path of waiting for history to provide an answer but to provide a solution from within our selves.

We conclude that real social progress can only arise through individual efforts by achieving the necessary financial education usually not taught in school. Instead, today, young people are taught to expect some strange incipient victory in life by either obtaining the "dream jobs" or winning the lottery.

No matter how smart we are, no matter how hard we work as employees, we will soon not be able to support our family, and we will not be able to help future generations out of our wage earnings.

We can start working on our asset portfolio today, no matter how small it is. Whatever we believe in, and no matter how much money we have, we can now grow our wealth by allowing technological improvements like artificial intelligence to propel our efforts. Archimedes once said, "Give me a lever long enough and a fulcrum on which to place it, and I shall move the world." We join a different class of people, those who have tools in addition to their sweat labor. Income growth in the 19th Century primarily occurred because of what we called the "robber barons" who attained great wealth by cutthroat competition or exploiting non-union labor. But today, enormous wealth is being generated by individuals who found a way to leverage new technologies, which have created entirely new industries practically overnight.

CHAPTER 6

Seven Investor Levels

Wealth requires the application of morals, mind, and money.

Nobody wants to be placed in a box. So, I apologize to the reader for presenting the investor levels in the following way. I discuss investor levels on the next few pages to provide a quick tool for finding out about your current ability to generate a wealth of generations. I designed these levels to give readers an initial idea about their financial habits and skills. I initially learned about the concept of investor levels from Robert Kiyosaki's book Cashflow Quadrant but have created a new meaning for each level. Level zero is the lowest level where everybody begins in life. Some start as children when they learn from their parents, while others learn in their jobs and from friends. Like any other skills and habits, the earlier in life we learn, the better we will get. I read that *The Beatles* were playing as young musicians in small clubs in Hamburg, Germany, seven nights a week from 08:30-09:30, 10:00 until 11:00, 11:30-12:30, and finished the evening playing from 01:00 until 02:00 in the morning for more than two years. That adds up to 4 hours a day, 365 days, two years equals 2,920 hours on stage during their time in Hamburg. Their musical performance became world-famous. As Malcolm Gladwell stated in his book, *Outliers* in 2008, the amount of time we practice a particular skill contributes to high success levels. He suggests that practicing for a total of 10,000 hours will make us experts.

Imagine that you dedicate that same amount of intense practice to your financial skills. You can discover many activities that you can practice regularly by downloading the Investor Level Table at www. ingemar-anderson.com. Please note that these investor levels have nothing to do with how much money you have (net worth equals all assets minus liabilities) or make (your income). The investor levels represent your state of mind and your habits that affect your financial decisions.

LEVEL 0

Individuals on level 0 don't have any money to invest. However, every individual has personal assets like skills and attributes that make that person valuable. Unfortunately, people on level 0 are unaware of any of their assets and seem to be stuck in their current financial realities. Individuals on level 0 pursue no activities that can be considered investing.

LEVEL 1

Level 1 individuals follow activities that we learn and practice in an average family today. These are paying bills on time, borrowing to buy a small house, purchasing consumer items, or going shopping. This level probably might be the most common in our society and is taught in primary school. Many people never move beyond this level in their lives. Even though the Investor Levels are not meant to be chronological, they represent the story of personal development for many people.

LEVEL 2

Level 2 activities are things that people typically learn the hard way during their first years in their jobs. They save money after their credit got ruined, build a savings account, save to buy rather than buy on credit, avoid credit card debt, and like security.

LEVEL 3

Individuals on level 3 start to learn investor skills and gain experience during their employment. For example, they begin using tax benefits when creating a 401(k) plan, buying company stocks or stock options offered by their employers, or participating in so-called flexible benefits programs with their employers.

Most level 3 investors are young employees or self-employed people like medical doctors, lawyers, and real estate agents. Young employees working for a medium or large company often have the advantage of learning on their jobs to work in a team and learn about investing from many different angles. In contrast, self-employed people tend to become very specialized, hence miss the opportunity to become a great investor, Level 4 and 5 investors.

Level 3 investors are still only buying financial products instead of creating financial products. They are still only using simple templates and readily available investment vehicles.

LEVEL 4

Level 4 investors have developed long-term investment plans. They occasionally work with Level 5 investors, and they start looking behind the curtains of financial products, and they start working on taking control of their financial assets.

Good examples of level 4 investors are white-collar employees in either management or other leading positions. Over the years, they have learned how to work in teams, create products, and sell them. For me, it does not matter what their professions are. They could be accountants, marketing gurus, salesmen, scientists, programmers, or designers. They must have learned how to be a good team player and lead a team.

LEVEL 5

Level 5 investors have typically passed the crowd that is working for money. They are mostly still employees, but they are not dependent on their salary. In 2003, Steve Jobs received an annual salary of one dollar, and many other CEO's have worked for that amount in the past. Some call these CEO's the "dollar-a-year-men." A typical Level 5 investor works as CEO of a company or a successful entrepreneur who either made millions by selling their company or owned one or more companies. Some see Level 5 investors as "The 5%" of our society. Most Level 5 investors often meet with level 6 investors.

Unfortunately, the overwhelming majority of the people today will never reach level 5 in their lifetime. It takes decades to learn level 5 skills, gain experience, and build a foundation of knowledge and habits. Only two types of people will master level 5: those who were educated and trained from their childhood and those who are self-made business people and investment gurus who have the urge, passion, professionalism, and patience to learn and apply good financial habits. But even these level 5 people are often not capable of transferring wealth to their kids and the following generations. Level 5 investors are very successful in business and investors with little understanding of *Wealth for Generations*.

LEVEL 6

Unfortunately, level 6 individuals are not always morally sound and mindful people in history. The Rockefeller family has been hated for many years for their ruthless and reckless behavior. Stories about John D. Rockefeller exist, which claim that he recklessly converted the entire world from a plant-based industry to a crude oil-based economy. Many people believe that he has suppressed the electric car's development, prevented Diesel engines from running on vegetable oil, and prohibited to run vehicles on alcohol-based fuels for years.

Rockefeller also knew that a new medical frontier opened up with the use of petrochemicals. Some historical sources claim that he forced doctors and hospitals to use petrochemicals instead of plant-based ingredients as the foundation for medicine, including aspirin, penicillin, and other treatment drugs. He expanded his medical empire by changing the plant-based homeopathic medicine to petro-chemical medicine domination.

His goal was to justify the modernization, streamlining, and consolidation of medical teaching in medical schools and hospitals. This effort forced out most of the teaching for plant-based homeopathic medicine. His actions changed the course of medicine in the western world. Many homeopathic schools were closed. Many hospitals had to change their direction from plant-based treatments. Some doctors were even jailed for not following the new regulation.

After 1913, all medical schools and hospitals, to receive Rockefeller grants and money, were directed to teach and do research in the directed medical areas where these newly discovered drugs could be patented and sold in the many drug outlets Rockefeller empire. This included Squibb, which, at the time, was a wholly-owned Rockefeller business.

In general, level 6 investors are individuals who grew up in wealth for generations. They are typically out of reach to the average citizen; they are not even known to the general public in most cases. Level 6 people are often referred to as "The 1%" of our society even though the actual number of people who are part of Level 6 families might only be a fraction of 1%. People on Investor Level 6 are considered "The Elite," and they are said to possess the following habits and skills:

- They are excellent stewards of money
- They generate sky-high passive income
- They own many globally strategic assets
- Their expenses are negligible compared to their income
- They control debt issuers
- They typically make other people rich
- They orchestrate other people
- They create megatrends
- They create financial products
- They always have several exit strategies
- They "always" win, they hate to lose
- They possess excessive cash
- They control their own and assets of others
- They work mostly behind curtains
- They invest in preferred stock
- They often make profits above 100%

People associated with *The Elite* do not typically appear in the media; they tend to make decisions behind closed doors. They and their forefathers have mastered the task of building wealth for generations. Those tasks include much more than financial education.

In America, level 6 investors come from families like the Rockefeller's, the Rothschild's in Europe and Asia, and the Oppenheimer's in Africa, to name a few. All these investors have in common that someone in their families founded ultra-successful businesses. In the last one hundred years or so, hundreds of such companies were founded, and the level 6 investor circle grew substantially. Today, the investor level 6 circle, or the Circle of The Elite, has several layers, and each has its power and influence, but we can expect that they all work together to achieve many goals, none of them we know about in detail. We should not ignore that many of level 6 families today might have direct or indirect access to federal agencies, determining many aspects of our personal lives.

But it seems to me that most people in these circles live in increasing alarm. They seem to be blinded by their successful involvement with the largest and most powerful corporations that already created never-seen technological possibilities in life science and microchip technology. Their involvement can create a New World for them, wholly detached from the rest of the people. They might even be afraid of ordinary people, so they prefer to avoid them. Their general education, habits, experience, and power are likely superior, so one might understand that they don't tend to hang out with us. Would you hang out with a bum? You might hand him or her a dollar or two. Investor level 6 individuals might see us, the average people, the same way we see a beggar.

Since investor level 6 people are highly connected, they can quickly form an alliance, which some people might consider as an evil alliance, or even as the Mark of the Beast or the Number of the Beast 666. The novel *The Time Machine* by H.G. Wells, George Orwell's 1984, or the book *The Hunger Games* by Suzanne Collins might exemplify what can happen when ordinary people stop caring about their future, and a select group of people suppresses them. These novels describe a world where elite-like units or corrupt people control everyone's life and take advantage of them.

I believe most individuals on investor level 6 and their families are very amiable people, and some in such high powers might be in a deep crisis today. They have excluded themselves from ordinary people so that they might lose contact with the real world. Natural resource production like crude oil and water might have reached a long-term peak output, so The Elite might feel their empire is in danger. A good example is how younger generations of level 6 investors feel and think nowadays. I recommend watching the documentarie *"The One Percent" and "Born Rich"* created by Jamie Johnson and Nick Kurzon. Jamie is the young heir to the Johnson & Johnson pharmaceutical fortune. Jamie and Nick created these documentaries in the early 2000s, which are available on YouTube. Search for the documentary film titles and their names Nick Kurzon and Jamie Johnson.

THE HOUSE OF THE ELITE

Sometimes, I see the current world as a giant house where every person in our society has its place. Individuals who live on top of the house are members of families who have built wealth over generations, and the members of these families today represent The Elite. They have been financially independent for decades. The people on level 5 are wealthy assistants of The Elite. Everybody below is dependent on the upper classes, who will scream for help from the higher levels when things get complicated.

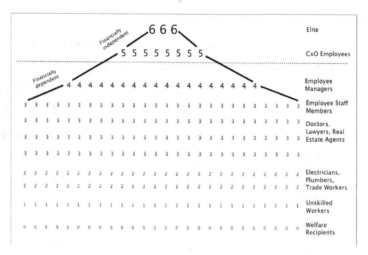

Figure: 6.2 The House of The Elite

#	Simple Name	Provocative Name	Spiritual Character*	Examples
0	Nothing-to-lose	Loser	Fight-or-Flight, The Hunted	Average worker or unemployed
1	Dreamer	Exploited	Reactive	Ambitious worker
2	Saver	Smarter consumer	Restful Awareness	Financially smarter workers
3	Speculator	Want-to-be Investor	Intuitive	Doctors, Artists, Scientists
4	Long-term investor	Part-time Investor	Creative	Many employees in leadership and management positions
5	Sophisticated investor	Active and passive investors	Visionary	Most CEOs, CFOs, etc., successful entrepreneurs, Elon Musk
6	Capitalist	Families with wealth of generation, The Elite	Sacred	Old Money like Rockefeller Family, Rothschild Family, and New Money like Bill Gates, Steve Jobs Family, Richard Branson, Warren Buffet

*Figure: 6.1 Investor Level Summary , *Spiritual Characters based on Deepak Chopra's book "The Seven Spiritual Laws of Success."*

INVESTOR LEVEL QUIZ

So, would you like to find out on which level you are based on this book? One easy way is to look at what 'you currently do for a living,' what your job is. Is your job one of the ones listed in the previous figure, or do you do something similar in your job? Your profession can be an excellent indicator of your investor level.

However, if you want to find out more about your current personal financial situation and your financial habits, complete the following exercise:

- Download the investor level table at https://www.ingemar-anderson.com. (see below QR code)
- Start with the first row and circle one habit that fits most of your personal situation.
- Repeat this until you get to the last row.
- After you made a circled in all rows, add up all investor levels you fall into, take the sum, and compare your total with the score at the bottom of the table.

SCAN ME

CHAPTER 7

The Division of Labor

"Let us conclude from these principles that nature creates some men for liberty and others for slavery; that it is useful and just that the slave should obey. The reader will perceive how exactly this passage is paralleled by the statements of middle-class economists, that incapacity, laziness, and thriftlessness will inevitably condemn a large portion of the population always to labor for a mere subsistence."

—Adam Smith, 1776

The above quote is what Adam Smith wrote in the introduction of his book *The Wealth of Nations*. I think this is a ruthless assessment of the situations of people who we might call employees today. However, many employees might feel precisely that way. In an earlier chapter, I described how a small portion of the country today owns and earns so much more money than the typical employee so that Adam Smith's statement may not be so far fetched.

There might always be many people who will have to work very hard for very little money. Emerging technologies like artificial intelligence or blockchain are putting more and more people out of work or require them to learn different, mostly white-collar skills. But this trend will be an opportunity for many to learn financial skills and become sophisticated investors. With the rise of new technology, the time is coming for people to break free from Adam Smith's terrible paradigm of *The Division of Labor*.

A VERY DIFFERENT CAREER STRATEGY

Life itself is all about the right mix of specialization and generalization, standardization, and individualism. It has been that way since the beginning of time. Beings with a high level of specialization were more effective than other creatures with less specialization. However, too many too specialized species went extinct when their environment changed too much, too fast.

So, being a highly specialized person might provide us with a lot of success, cash, and a decent salary. However, we might lose our job overnight if nobody needs our skills anymore. I have seen many smart people who became highly trained, specialized individuals working in their field for several years and have saved a considerable amount of money during that period. They prepared for the day when their specialization was no longer needed or when they were ready to do something else. But others were not; they have often not saved enough money to sustain a career transition.

WHY NOT BE A FISHERMAN FOR A WHILE?

I have some friends who were fisherman for several years when they were younger. They worked on a ship far out at sea sometimes for three or four months in a row. When they returned on shore, they would receive a paycheck that exceeded many other people's annual salary. After being fishermen for several years, they earned enough money to pay cash for several condominiums, fourplexes, and other income-producing assets. These assets then produced enough income for them to cover more than their monthly living expenses. Many of these friends are now successful businessmen, investors, and advisors.

Fortunately, we are all highly flexible and intelligent beings who can change and adapt to different environments. Like the fishermen, some people can even use these human attributes to benefit by taking advantage of highly specialized skills to make enough money to be then able to pursue other things.

Adam Smith already foresaw the essence of industrialism in his book "The Wealth of Nations" by determining that labor division represents an increase in productivity. For Smith, specialization of labor was the dynamic engine of economic progress. And he must have been right. Most would agree that the last two or three centuries' worldwide economic development is a unique success story in human history. However, in a further chapter of the same book, Smith criticizes labor division by writing that labor specialization leads to a 'mental mutilation' in workers.

Today we know that there are limits to labor specialization. I even suggest that the current employment system requires white-collar and blue-collar workers to be too specialized for an extended period, in many cases, an entire work life. A few would argue that this is the cause of all kinds of distortions in our society, leading to extremely high divorce rates, social isolation, mental mutilation and decadence, and certain extremist behaviors.

This book could provide solutions to solve the problem of such an over-specialization. I believe the time is here for a more sophisticated view on employment, entrepreneurship, and 'investorship.'

DO YOU STILL WORK FOR MONEY?

Can you imagine a world where people do not work for money but experience only? My impression is that being employed is the hobby of the 'rich' and the curse of the 'poor.' What if employment could be everyone's hobby? For example, I know great musicians whose hobby is playing and sell music, and they do so with more success than some other people who play professionally. In particular, one friend of mine inherited a blacksmith business from his father that he had little interest in pursuing. However, instead of turning away from the company or selling it, he decided to work with his father for several years in the business. Later, he took over the business and today let his employees manage it.

Meanwhile, he pursued a career in music and now makes more money with his own record company than his father's business ever did. Now, he owns two very successful companies. The point I am making is that if his father did not have a business, he might not have been able to become a successful musician. When he was younger, he did not need to work, working was a hobby for him, but he learned how to run a business. And making music was his passion, which, like his dad did with his company, turned his passion into a business.

THE WORLD WILL BE A BETTER PLACE

Would the world not be a much better place if we all had the chance to pursue our dreams like my friend? Can you see what would happen if people inherited income-producing assets like small businesses or real estate from their parents instead of liabilities like homes or cars that are not paid off in most cases? What would happen if retirees lived from income, which comes from their income-producing asset instead of accumulated 401(k) money that will very likely be all used up when they die? What would happen, if people asked themselves how much income per month they needed to retire instead of how much money they needed in the bank account?

In a financially sophisticated world, our kids would be able to work for experience instead of money. And what if we could even teach our kids how to create real income-producing assets that generated real value every month? They could not only live from these assets, but they would also be able to contribute valuable work and knowledge to produce even more valuable assets.

This book is written for everybody interested in breaking free from the traditional economic thinking driven by the division of labor principles. It is written for people who like to look behind the curtain of the current financial system to see a world that is not dependent upon money but instead creates utility and value.

PART TWO

MIND

CHAPTER 8

The Mindset of an Investor

"The heaviest penalty for declining to rule is to be ruled by someone inferior to yourself." —Plato, **THE REPUBLIC**

CLASS STRUCTURE IN THE MODERN WORLD

One of the erroneous beliefs in America today is that social classes don't exist anymore. A moment of reflection will immediately show that significant income discrepancies exist in America today. The top 1% of American households dominate the ownership of most corporations. Whereas, working-class people very seldom own any publicly traded entities. Even when working people begin to enter the class of entrepreneurs, it is usually at the level of small business in the form of individual proprietorships. Young people are even less likely to own their own business. Many are saddled with huge student loan payments and can barely afford to begin young adult life with the purchase of a home and family raising.

The table is tilted against the bottom 99%. What are the causes of this "tilt?"

- People are pushed into relying on credit for their daily consumption needs.
- Financial sophistication is not taught in school.
- Corporations for their cheap labor are exploiting young people.
- There is a tendency for the next higher micro class to keep those below in 'their place.'

- The larger the business entity the more likely it is to be able to purchase in large quantities and also to engage in price wars with competitors – the leverage of business of scale.
- People dependent primarily on salary income are limited by the number of hours per week that they can work.
- The logic of automation – machines are cheaper than people.
- Most people are not prepared for their needs after retirement.

EMERGING AS AN INVESTOR

We might not see our self as an investor, or we might even dislike thinking about investing at all. However, this might be a fatal mistake. All of us make daily decisions about what to buy, what we trade, what we learn, and what we spend our time on. Everybody has financial obligations and some source of income. And everybody can decide, daily, how to manage each of these factors.

Over the last few decades, too many of us seem to have forgotten to be and act as investors. Too many of us became super consumers, dreamers, borrowers, financial losers, pumped up with literally unlimited money from the central banks. In the twentieth century, the middle class grew to be the largest group in our society, which spurred economic growth through ever-increasing consumption. That has been a good thing for all. But the times have come where the middle class, the lucky ones, found their spot in our overall wealthy nation and became more and more threatened by the instability of the same system that brought the middle class to where it is today: the current economic system. Many people in the middle class have either down-shifted and now work fewer hours, or they were downsized and needed to find new employment that requires them to work longer hours.

INVESTOR LEVELS AND SOCIAL CLASSES

The ongoing down-shifting of individuals from the middle class resulted in a unique phenomenon: we are coming apart, as Charles Murray claims in his book Coming Apart. Charles explains that a moral decline combined with the rise of poverty within the middle class creates a more divided society.

For me, part of the moral decline is also the decline of well-rounded financial education and sophistication. The following diagram consists of nine boxes. Every single box represents a unique financial situation from low to high wealth combined with the financial literacy from level 0 to level 6 of a person. For example, in the lower-left box are individuals who have no wealth and are not financially sophisticated.

Important to note is that I define wealth as passive income over personal expenses: $W = P / E$. We can increase our wealth when we raise our passive income or decrease our personal expenses.

Individuals seem to hang out around certain investor levels and wealth levels, as illustrated by the nine boxes. However, family values, faith, vocation, and community increasingly seem to separate the nine groups of people from each other. For that reason, these groups represent certain social classes.

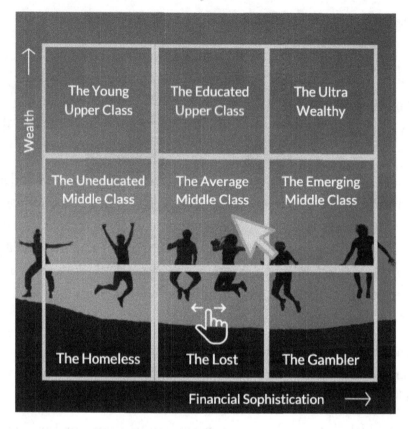

Figure: 8.1 The modern classes in our society.

HOW ARE YOU BEING TREATED?

Have you noticed that service companies like wireless communication service companies, hotel chains, banks, or credit card companies seem to cater progressively to only some of these classes because each class has very different needs? Have you ever noticed how a representative from American Express communicates with you over the phone versus someone from, let's say Citibank? Have you ever experienced how you are treated as a private client in a bank versus an average bank customer?

When individuals become financially more literate, they move from their current investor level to a higher level, and at the same time, they might become part of the next group to their right. For example, it is a well-known phenomenon that when a person in the working class pursues a better education, he or she will likely get many new friends in the middle class and might even break with his or her past life.

If you are an average investor, someone in the middle class, and if you like to improve your financial literacy, you need to change your habits, get a lot of investing experience, increase your financial skills and education. You will need friends from the higher investor levels that can coach you.

There are only very few people who are part of two classes on the same investor level. For example, on investor level 2, there are people from the working class and some few people from the middle class. They all have comparable financial habits, skills, and education. However, from their upbringing, heritage, or other reasons, consider themselves either in the working class or in the middle class. The same is true for a few people on investor level 5. Some people from the middle class on level 5 have excellent financial knowledge and skills, so they are sometimes able to join up with individuals from people in The Elite.

I wrote this book for people who are willing to go with me on that rough and cumbersome journey that takes us from the lowest investor level to a higher investor level. It requires discipline, patience, and time. But I want to point out that we won't need any additional money for that journey. The journey will instead lead us through wild lifestyle changes, mindset transformations, and colossal paradigm shifts.

In my observations, all three groups, the working class, the middle class, and The Elite, avoid each other like the plague. They are entirely incompatible, except some individuals at edges of the investor level bell curves. Today, these different groups have mostly nothing in common except their basic needs. For an individual, it is becoming more challenging to move from one group to another. And, as described earlier, these classes seem to grow apart more and more.

The typical reader of this book is most likely interested in becoming a level 5 investor. An individual on investor level 5 or 6 is an inside investor (not to be confused with an inside trader!). He or she works beyond the visible economic system. They have a network of many other level 5 and 6 friends. They have abundant social capital since they all work as a team to put mega-deals together. It is indeed a very exclusive crowd. Many of them appear on television here and there or are mentioned in the financial news. They don't want to play with the average investors, which are still in the financial rat race. For example, in Germany, there is one percent that owns more financial assets than 90% of the rest of the population, the middle and working class, who are in the financial rat race, where their total passive income is lower than their total expenses.

WHO DO YOU HANG OUT WITH?

In short: investors on different investor levels typically don't want to *play* with each other. Who do you hang out with? Can you assign individual boxes to some of your friends using the diagram before?

DO I LIVE IN A BUBBLE?

So, it seems there are entirely separate groups or classes in our society that don't even really talk to each other. You might be an average investor on level 3 or 4, and if you like to speak to sophisticated, accredited investors, you need to learn the language of level 5 and 6 investors. Have you ever met one? Would they talk to you? And why? Before you try to reach out to such people, you will have to learn to speak their language, understand their motivations. You will very likely not agree with many of their beliefs and actions, and you might even oppose their thinking altogether. Not everyone is made for a world on investor levels 5 and 6. However, I ask you to think about this from this point of view. If we, as ordinary people, let the 5% of level 5 people and 1% of level 6 people do what they are doing without even interacting with the ordinary people, they will do whatever they want. I claim that becoming a sophisticated level 5 investor, which means interacting and being able to communicate with the 5% and 1% on the same level, becomes not only an individual quest for freedom but an obligation for the common good and future generations.

The mental states of individuals on investor levels 5 and 6 operate outside of the visible economic structure. By that, they play by different rules: different tax laws apply to them, they have different purchasing and negotiation power, and they enjoy various benefits at banks and other institutions. They even have very different lifestyles and values than other people.

ENTITLEMENT

It is easy to understand that individuals on level 5 and 6 who receive much more significant benefits get used to these treatments, and the chances are high that they will lose contact with the average investors. They then seem to live in a bubble.

Such a bubble explains why there are even stronger forces that change the typical middle class towards a more dual society: *the rich get richer and the poor get poorer.*

This trend will continue unless average investors take action and become more sophisticated in their financial education, lifestyle, and values like family, faith, community, and their choices of habits.

HOW DO WE START?

There are only two things we need to become financially more sophisticated, and that is patience and discipline. Pick a trade, a skill, or an asset that you are passionate about, and then use an excellent opportunity to start a business.

We can still live the American Dream these days, overcome the hurdles, and go on the path from being financially powerless to the average investor and a sophisticated investor. To become an average investor we need financial education. To become a sophisticated investor, you need even more financial knowledge and vast business and investment experience to buy or start successful companies that provide us with that excessive cash, which we need to invest. Excessive cash sounds funny or too much to ask for. However, cash will pour in, like from a water hose if we have a sound business system. We will use that cash from our business to invest in assets that the average investor has no access to. This is how sophisticated investors do it. Once we have excessive cash, people will find us faster than we might wish for, and they will offer us cool investment deals that we have never thought about.

The most comfortable and practical path to becoming a sophisticated investor is through becoming a business owner first, then using the excess cash generated by our business to invest in other assets.

For the longest time, I did not understand this concept, even after reading several books about investing, I did not know how to start. Slowly, I discovered that becoming a sophisticated investor is a very long process and that I had to change many things in my life first before I can even try to become a sophisticated investor.

I had an excellent education. I had a bachelor's degree and a master's degree in finance. I knew all the theory, but I was not street-smart in a financial sense. When I started my new career as an investor, I felt like a kid who graduated from school, starting a new job even though I have worked as an employee for almost twenty years.

But eventually, two things got me started: I founded my first company in 2008, and I studied the tax laws much more extensively. Since then, I have started an investment company, software and service company, and a publishing company with great success.

Looking back, I realized that I grew up in a state where many people are financially exceptionally sophisticated. The region is the economically most prosperous country in Europe: Germany, and it is the wealthiest state in Germany, where I grew up: Bavaria. Their secret is to promote small businesses. Here is a Bavarian Fairy Tale from ABC News in February 2012. ABC News reported in its Foreign Correspondent section on February 14, 2012:

"Fact is Bavaria is the richest state in Germany and Germany is now the richest country in Europe. And while much of the rest of Europe is mired in the financial quicksand of a sovereign debt crisis, business in Bavaria is booming, exports are rising, and unemployment is at a 20-year low".

How come? Well, the Germans have got a word for it, which is a concept that pervades their general approach to doing business. It is basically just another word for medium sized businesses, partnerships or S corporations: *Mittelstand*. The German secret to the success of modest family enterprises is saturation of the economy with small businesses. Auto-giants like Audi and BMW are examples of small businesses that made it all the way to the global domination. They call it *Mittelstand*. In other European countries and even in America, the word "*Mittelstand*" became a known term for its very strong small business entrepreneurship. The French even speak of "Le Mittelstand'" and recently announced to copy that idea to promote small businesses. Many say a strong Mittelstand is one reason why Germany has a very strong middle class, many successful companies and many of the wealthiest people in the world.

But will all these initiatives to build a strong Mittelstand be successful? The answer is no if there are not enough people on investor levels 5 and 6. If there are too few people who understand how to start and run a business and understand why it is so important to invest in good assets, then there will be no Mittelstand.

INVESTING IS LIKE HUNTING

Investing is a hunting game, not a shopping game. We need ammunition, which is represented by readily available cash, and we need a whole bunch of experience to catch a wild animal successfully. Now we also know why it is essential to keep money in cash (some call keeping cash saving money). So, when we see a deer, we want to have our ammunition ready and shoot quickly. When we see an excellent asset, we want to have our cash prepared to buy rapidly under the best terms possible. Paying with cash will get us the best deal, and chances are much higher to generate good income with that asset.

FREEING MY MIND!

A sophisticated investor can step out of his shoes and detach himself from his personal life. The reason why this step is necessary is that he needs to manage his personal finance and his investment completely separately. The average investor confronted with investment opportunities typically reaches into his savings or personal line of credit to finance the purchase of the asset. Instead, I am suggesting that the sophisticated investor reaches out to other funding sources rather than their own funding or banks. To list a few, they can do that by:

- Organizing fundraising events

- Writing books to raise awareness and funds from royalties.
- Joining service clubs in your community (like Rotary Clubs) in their towns
- Working closely with the local Chamber of Commerce

CHAPTER 9

Five Types of Asset Classes

When I start thinking I will stop paying.

Based on my observations, almost all financial education taught in school and college today seems to be very technical. I remember the classes I took in my MBA program, which was loaded with countless scientific studies and analyses of sophisticated financial vehicles. In my real-life experience, financial sophistication and success are much simpler than what we learn in school and from the media today. It starts with the question, *"does an asset make me richer today or not?"* In today's world, we study more the characteristics of financial products like currencies, stocks, funds, or bonds instead of learning how to create financial products.

This book reveals we need to know how to create financial products. The most important term we need to know before we even start investing is the term *asset class*. This chapter will give an overview of the five major asset classes if you are not familiar with the term asset class.

You might have learned about asset classes in the past, and you might own and manage assets already in different asset classes. There are only five major asset classes: securities, businesses, commodities, real estate, and the money market. So, if you like to diversify your portfolio, these are your choices.

But there is one basic rule: before you invest in a particular asset class, make sure you know the asset class in and out. Many great investors are kings of their asset classes. For example, Leonard Norman Stern has been viewed as an expert in real estate since the 1970s. Warren Buffet has always been the king of stock markets. Matthew Simmons was king of commodities, and Steve Jobs is known as a business entrepreneur who made many companies like Apple Inc. and Pixar ultra-successful companies.

Asset Class	Examples	Type
Money Market	Currencies, Cash, Bank Accounts, CDs, etc.	Paper Asset
Securities	Equities (Stocks), Bonds	Paper Asset
Businesses	Royalties, Patents, Businesses	Hard Asset
Commodities	Precious Metals, Crude Oil, Agriculture	Hard Asset
Real Estate	Residential, Commercial	Hard Asset

Figure 9.1 Asset Classes

Most people only own securities and assets in the money market. These asset classes are mostly easy to understand and easy to trade. On the other hand, there are two asset classes, businesses, and real estate, which are challenging to understand and challenging to buy and sell. Hence, not many people own businesses or real estate. However, holding companies and real estate assets can generate the most significant income. There is an inverse relationship between asset income and the number of people who invest in certain asset classes today. The higher the return, the fewer people invest in these assets. The reason is that asset classes with potential high-income opportunities require much higher skill sets than asset classes that provide lower returns. Most financial advisors make the connection between high financial return and higher risk. They generally do not mention that the investor can eliminate almost all risk by increasing their knowledge about the asset.

There are several seminars and classes you can visit for all five asset classes. By attending such workshops, you can find out if you like these assets and have a passion for them. An excellent way to find groups for each asset class is to use social media like meetup.com or online courses. But please remember, visiting these seminars will only be the entry point for you. Before you invest in an expensive asset, you need more skills and experience, which you can only gain from starting small. Buy a small condo for income, park that money for a while in low risk, low return securities. Then, leave some of your income in the money market to have cash readily available when you have the opportunity to buy another real estate property or even a cash flow positive business.

MONEY MARKET

The money market consists of mainly savings accounts, checking accounts, foreign currency accounts, cash deposits, and cash.

You don't need much experience and knowledge when you get into the money market. Hence this market is by far the most common asset class. Almost everyone has a checking account at a bank.

However, it is important to understand that assets in the money market are only a medium of exchange. As Jeff Naber from Nabers Financials says about paper money: *"notes are just some weird little papers with dead presidents on them, and people actually would rather work for real stuff that you can exchange these little papers for. Currency is not the real economy. The things you exchange paper money for are the real economy, which is one of the most important realizations any investor should have."* Real assets are commodities and businesses that can produce income. The currency is not the value; the item being exchanged for cash is the value. While the entire money market can collapse, real assets will still be there. As an investor, you want to hold many tangible assets. Money market assets are useful to store wealth for a specific time until you find a lucrative hard investment.

SECURITIES

Securities are paper assets like stocks, bonds, ETF's, other funds, and certificates. Securities and money market assets are under the same umbrella term. Investors can exchange them for other paper assets or assets in other asset classes. Holdings in the money market and the security market are excellent assets for storing wealth. They represent an easy way to exchange value. Cash is king! Securities are riskier than money but can provide a tremendous long-term financial return.

If you only invest in the money and security market, your assets might not be diversified enough to create long-term wealth for generations. Today, most retirement assets consist entirely of investments in paper assets. In a later chapter, I will write more about retirement planning strategies.

BUSINESSES

Becoming a business owner today is easier than ever. And thanks to automation and software support, running a business does not require an armada of employees.

A business owner is not a self-employed person. Being a business owner includes much more than just providing services in return for money. Having started two successful businesses from scratch, I have seen what it means to be a business owner. Most important: you need a business blueprint, which explains how a business can be scaled to any size. The blueprint also needs to show how to solve real problems for your customers. You might be the only employee of your business for a particular time. Still, the important thing is that you have a blueprint, a system that can generate income without you being involved later on, and that can be scaled to almost any size. That income can come from selling products or services, royalties from a book you wrote, or patents and trademarks you submitted.

REAL ESTATE

Like businesses, real estate is also a tangible asset in the economy. When you buy a property, the first and foremost question you should ask yourself is if you plan for portfolio income or passive income from tenants. Will the property's rent income be a source of recurring revenue, or do you expect the property to go up in value in a foreseeable time? Or do you intend to flip the property by remodeling it and selling it with a profit?

Either way, you should educate yourself about the fundamentals of real estate. Real estate is a unique asset class, which has a lot of pitfalls. You have to consider many factors if you want to make an excellent real estate deal. You need to do a detailed cash flow analysis and determine the right leverage with bank loans, which I will explain later in the book. Even proper financing might not save you from a bad deal. You have to consider that not every bank will give you a loan for certain kinds of properties. You have to get knowledgeable about city planning and zoning changes in your county or city. Also, there are many opportunities to reduce your taxes through real estate. In my experience, you can make money in four areas in real estate: cash flow, appreciation, tax benefits, principal reductions. You will find more information about real estate investment in chapter Asset Development.

Before you decide to invest your time in real estate, and before you purchase your first property, you need to find out which type of real estate suits your investment style. All real estate types are very different and require very different skills. For example, think about what kinds of tenants you want to focus on: long-term tenants with families, students, or short-time renters like Airbnb customers, young or older individuals, or smaller companies requiring office space.

COMMODITIES

Commodities are the fifth asset class I describe in this book. They are not paper assets like securities or money market assets, and they are also not like real estate and businesses since they do not generate any income. Commodities are in between paper assets and tangible assets. On the one hand, they do not represent a value based on a financial product like all paper assets. On the other hand, they do not produce income like businesses and real estate. Commodities serve a different purpose: they primarily provide the investor with security. The value of a commodity will typically never go to zero, and can, in some cases, provide a source of physical safety for self-usage.

When I talk about commodities for investing purposes, I do mean actual physical goods. The USA's most known commodity exchange markets are the NYMEX and COMEX, where investors and traders can exchange energy, precious metals, and industrial metals. Other exchange markets like the Memphis Cotton Exchange or the Minneapolis Grain Exchange specialize in agricultural products like wheat, barley, sugar, maize, cotton, cocoa, coffee, milk products, pork bellies, etc. Besides, many commodity investors buy physical instances of a commodity like gold or silver and store them in their safes. The advantage of owning physical commodities typically means better access to it when in need. Still, self-storage might not outweigh the disadvantage of higher storage costs, higher risks of being robbed, and more effort to trade them. To eliminate these disadvantages, you can check out new services that have emerged in the last few years, allowing companies and individual investors to trade digital tokens representing physical gold via blockchain transactions.

You can always hire commodity brokers and asset management companies. These companies are specialized in trading commodities and often provide low-risk trades with high yields.

THE INVESTMENT CYCLE

Level 5 and 6 investors play in all five asset classes. They might have their focus on one asset class. However, the advantage of using all asset classes is that the investor can benefit from all asset classes' characteristics. They are applying a two-bucket investment approach, which is a pretty simple concept. You create two virtual buckets in your portfolio: the paper assets bucket and the hard asset bucket. Now, you take the paper asset bucket, which you have to fill up initially from your salary or any other income you might have, and pour it into the hard asset bucket. In other words, you buy real estate, start or buy businesses or commodities using your money in the bank, selling securities or bonds. Automatically, the money will flow back from your income-producing hard assets into the paper asset bucket, and you can pour the paper money again back into the hard asset bucket. The income from your hard assets, your real assets, will provide you with income in the form of money market assets (currency, money), which you can reinvest in hard assets.

Robert Kiyosaki sums this simple cycle up as: *"I have a problem with too much money. I can't reinvest it fast enough, and because I reinvest it, more money comes in. Yes, the rich do get richer."*

If you are serious about building a real nest egg for your future, your retirement, or if you like to leave your children with real assets, you will have to think like a level 5 or level 6 investors and follow the 2-bucket investment approach as illustrated in the following figure.

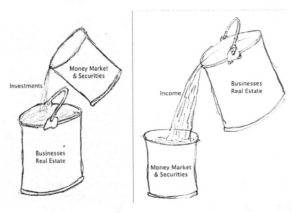

*Figure: 9.2 Investing liquid assets in real assets (left),
Receiving income from hard assets (right)*

A business is the most effective asset class in terms of income generation. It can generate that excessive amount of cash, which you need to invest in other assets. Even Warren Buffet, who initially made most of his money in the security market, is now heavily invested in businesses like the BNSF Railway Company. He owns and runs Berkshire Hathaway, with a market capitalization of over 500 billion dollars and earnings of over 80 billion dollars in 2018.

Asset Class	Asset Type	PORTFOLIO / PASSIVE	Typical Income
Money Market	Paper Asset	Portfolio Income	Capital gains, interest
Securities	Paper Asset	Portfolio Income	Capital gains, dividends
Commodities	Real Asset	Portfolio Income	Capital gains
Real Estate	Real Asset	Passive Income	Rent income
Businesses	Real Asset	Passive Income	Net income from business operations and dividends

Figure: 9.3 Overview of all five Asset Classes

CRYPTOCURRENCY

Should you invest in cryptocurrency? Cryptocurrency is a new phenomenon that started in 2009 with a groundbreaking development called blockchain. Bitcoin is one application of a vastly evolving blockchain technology and can be traded easily using smartphone apps or online services like blockchain.com. It is the most traded cryptocurrency today and has reached incredible gains since its inception in 2009. If you bought one bitcoin in 2009, you would own over 10,000 dollars if you sold that bitcoin today. Of course, it is still speculative where the value of bitcoin will go, but experts are excited about the entire blockchain development and have high hopes in a cryptocurrency that can increase trust between buyers and sellers. Cryptocurrencies are part of the asset class money market and will play a significant role in our economy. However, it is premature to rely only on the growth and availability of this new currency.

ARE ART AND COLLECTIBLES ASSETS?

Art as an asset is much debated, and some might say they are also very risky. Someone I know calls art just 'broken things' as the artist used fresh paint and a nice white canvas to make both unusable. But if you have a passion for collectibles, art can be for you, and depending who owned the pieces of art in the past; it might cash out very well if needed. However, art and collectibles are very speculative. I am not recommending putting art into your asset portfolio until you have so much cash at hand that you can pay for a particular piece of art or a scarce collectible item with your petty cash.

ARE NATURAL GOODS AN ASSET CLASS?

In economically challenging times, natural goods like food items, items for your hygiene, or even seeds and fresh vegetables from your garden might become the biggest asset you own. When you plan your financial freedom, you should not underestimate the importance of natural goods if you lose all your financial assets. A stock and your supply of natural products can lower your expenses and help others in need. However, this book will not get more into natural goods as assets beyond this paragraph.

A WORD ABOUT DERIVATIVES

Warren Buffet says, "Derivatives are financial weapons of mass destruction." And a statistic published by GlobalResearch.ca reports that derivatives were worth more than twenty times the world GDP in 2012.

The basic idea of derivatives is to increase the leverage for the derivative issuer, who is a sophisticated investor. With every other financial asset than derivatives, you buy a share of the actual asset, like stock from a company you own a particular share of that company. However, derivatives are financial instruments in the form of contracts (options, forward contracts, futures, etc.) that allow investors to speculate on the future price of, for example, commodities or shares —without buying the underlying investment.

SO, WHY ARE DERIVATIVES SO DANGEROUS?

Derivatives are legal contracts that are made between adults, and they are like WMDs, as Warren Buffet says. Since derivatives tend to amplify the power of underlying financial products and commodities, they can quickly derail a particular type of asset class or specific economic sectors. Even though derivatives are not part of the real economy, they can manipulate the financial system and destabilize it. This book does not cover derivatives in more detail since derivatives tend to be investment vehicles for professional speculators who do not invest in passive income but for capital gains only.

CHAPTER 10

Why does Wealth Only Trickle up?

Entrepreneurs work for free. Poor people work for money.

The wealthy get richer, and the poor get poorer. That is a phenomenon long observed, and now Thomas Piketty documented and verified this situation very well in his book *Capital in the 21st Century*. Piketty explains this phenomenon with a tendency of the investment rate of return (r) that exceeds the economic growth rate of a country (g): r > g. This phenomenon, he says, leads to a concentration of wealth, and hence to inequality of income.

Thomas Piketty seems to avoid the discussion about how to improve this situation, but he says that there are many forces and measurements like taxation that can change this growing gap. One approach that I have not heard discussed anywhere yet is to close the gap approaching it from the bottom instead of the top. In my opinion, the high rate of return that all these sophisticated investors are receiving is not the problem. The problem is the low return (g) that ordinary people are achieving.

Let me explain. Just a few centuries ago, only a fraction of the citizens were able to read or write. The gap between the wealthy royal establishment and the poor people was at a rate unimaginable today. But now in the Twenty-first Century, nearly everybody is literate, and wealth has indeed trickled up and created a strong middle-class. I suggest that our current generation can achieve the same in financial literacy that our ancestors gained for reading and writing literacy. I am sure that we can gradually close the gap between return (r) and growth (g).

INVESTMENT STYLES

Because investment styles vary from investor to investor, from investment to investment and will also change with different overall economic situations, you should familiarize yourself with the different ways to manage your assets. Your style might change after certain economic events, growth periods, and recessions and especially during and after depressions. In below figure are eight basic characteristics of investment styles.

Characteristic	A	B	C
Time	Short Term	Mid Term	Long Term
Risk	Risk Averse	Risk Tolerant	Risk Seeker
Capitalization (Cap)	Small Cap	Mid Cap	Big Cap
Derivatives	Low	Medium	High
International Diversification	National	Regional	Global
Asset Class Diversification	Low	Medium	High
Investor Involvement	Low	High	Medium
Businesses	Value	Growth	Quality

Figure: 10.1 Investment Styles Summary

THREE TYPES OF INVESTORS

Amongst average investors are three types. The saver focuses all activities on saving money and sometimes buys assets at the lowest price possible. The speculator focuses on the biggest bang for the buck with little or no knowledge about the assets. The specialist, however, only buys assets after a very detailed due diligence process and keeps very well informed about the asset after asset acquisition.

The specialist picks a particular asset class and becomes the absolute steward of that asset class. The specialist is on its way to becoming a sophisticated investor.

Type	Paraphrase
Saver	Slow grower
Speculator	The shotgun investor
Specialist	The vertical investor

Figure: 10.2 Three common types of investors

A WORD ABOUT MARKET MANIPULATIONS

It is no secret that the level 5 and 6 investors can manipulate specific markets to their benefit. For example, while a group of sophisticated investors meets at a particular location like a golf course, they discover their passion for a specific asset, like stock or a commodity. At one point, they happen to agree to invest in the same asset. Of course, it is very natural that they would also talk about when they plan to invest in it. Consequently, they might even buy on the same day or week. If their purchases are big enough within a relatively small market like the precious metals market, the effect might be that the asset's price on the purchase day will shoot up. There are all kinds of techniques on how to manipulate the market. When you enter "market manipulation" in Google News search, you might be overwhelmed with examples of incidents and cases pursued by the SEC.

Market manipulation is an ugly thing, and nobody wants to talk about it. Sometimes investors might not even really be aware of how much they manipulate the market with their investment transaction. But every investor has to deal with such manipulations at one point in time. Smaller and bigger manipulations do happen more often than one would think. Market manipulations occur in any asset class, and they are prohibited in most countries. If you are interested, you will find numerous famous cases of market manipulation, which I encourage you to identify and study yourself since it helps you understand more about the market in general. You, as an average investor should know about these possibilities of market manipulation. It would help if you were cautious when you buy an asset and consider the impact on your assets. One rule to always remember is: the smaller the market for an asset, the easier it is to manipulate the market price by buying or selling significant amounts of that asset.

Asset Type—Category	Typical Management Activities
Real Estate—Income	Condo Maintenance, Repairs, Tenants, Accounting
Real Estate—Flipping	Find, Fund and Flip (The 3 F's)
Securities—Stocks	Monitor Stock Price and company news
Securities—Funds	Research, Hope and Pray
Government Bonds	Watch Government and overall economic events
Commodities	Watch economic activities, growth and GDP
Money Market	Park money and find investment opportunity in real estate, business and commodities.

Figure: 10.3 Asset Types and their typical management activities

CHAPTER 11

The Two Laws of Wealth

"Wealth consists not in having great possessions, but in having few wants."—Epictetus AD c. 55 – 135

The above quote from the Greek philosopher Epictetus recapitulates the idea mentioned in the introduction to this volume that wealth is the excess of means over needs. This approach ensures that one can always meet their needs in a timely fashion. Who would not like to be wealthy?

Everyone recalls the old story of the genie of the magic lamp. The genie promises to fulfill three wishes. Most people imagining themselves with this opportunity would make their first wish for wealth. The wise person would wish first for health because without health. The money would be of little use. Notice here, though, that there is a distinction between wish and will. Wishing is the mere desire that something will happen. Until we can translate dreams into decisions, we have nothing accomplished. The German word "wollen" comes much closer than the English word "will." Wollen has with it a connotation of what in English we would call willpower, and willpower, in turn, is more than desire, it is a wellspring of decisiveness and vigor that plunges ahead into life.

The French word for this concept is "elan vital." During the early years of the 20th century and particularly during WW I, the belligerents often spoke of what was then called "national will." The belief was that granted equality in numbers of soldiers and arms, that nation would prevail that had the greatest desire for victory. I wish to appeal to more objective factors than a mere intense desire for supplementary means as the road to wealth. But without desire and decisiveness, any formula that I might supply would lack the requisite decisiveness and commitment, which are necessary if wealth is to be obtained.

THE FIRST LAW OF WEALTH

The components of what I call the First Law for Wealth have three parts: Wealth, Passive Income, and Personal Expenses. I define Wealth W as total monthly passive income P from the assets you own over personal total monthly expenses E.

The formula for the *First Law of Wealth* is:

$$Wealth = \frac{PassiveIncome}{Expenses + PassiveIncome}$$

As a result, if your passive income is zero, then your wealth score is simply zero, based on the First Law of Wealth.

SOME EXAMPLES

Tim has no passive income and 2,000 dollars of expenses every month. His Wealth Score is simply zero based on the Wealth Formula.

On the other hand, Rose receives a 2,000 dollar check from a fund for life, and her expenses are 1,500 dollars every month. Her Wealth Score is 0.57. A score above 0.5 means that all expenses can be covered using passive income. Rose can, but she does not need to work for money to cover her costs.

I define wealth as the ability to meet all expenses with passive income in a time as they come due over a lifetime. That is all very well and good, but of course, it makes no provision for an excess that can pass on to the new generation. For this book, I define wealth as the ratio between your passive income and the amount you need to cover all reasonable personal lifetime expenses plus your passive income.

REASONABLE EXPENSES

Note that I said "reasonable expenses." Adam Smith quotes in his book *The Wealth of Nations Xenophon of Oikonomikos*. He writes in the introduction that wealth is a relative *thing*:

> *"A man's wealth is only what benefits him. Suppose a man used his money to buy a mistress by whose influence his body, his soul, and his household would be all made worse, how could we then say that his money was of any advantage to him?*
>
> *We may then exclude money also from being counted as wealth, if it is in the hands of one who does not know how to use it."*

This whole question of miss-spent wealth should recall to your mind at this point what we had to say in the early chapters of this book about the moral foundation of wealth. How many people, who society calls wealthy, use their excess means to acquire pseudo-goods or services that only succeed in ruining their lives. Not only are such needs often addictive, but they also bring in its train many misfortunes. A willful man might only be a stubborn man who is unwilling to learn from humanity's collective wisdom. The experiment of humankind shows that a man poor in material wealth but rich in virtue is superior to a man with significant material assets but with a foolish mind.

Surpluses begin when an individual feels a sense of wellbeing at his current level of expenditure. What we call the virtue of thrift is for a person to reach a state of wellbeing at a low level of relative spending. We call a spendthrift of a wastrel, a person who continues to spend beyond the point where most people would be satisfied with their state in life. We can find most people somewhere between these two points.

WHAT ABOUT LIVING EXPENSES?

Technology that provides goods and services to accommodate our basic and social needs are becoming more efficient every year. LED lights have drastically reduced the money we need to spend on electricity to light our homes and businesses. Most electric devices are now using considerably less energy than just 20 years ago. Smart electronics help us find information to save on energy and find better deals. Furthermore, energy generation through solar and other sources makes us less dependent on other companies that used to increased our monthly expenses.

I predict that the average household will lower their expenses drastically within the next ten years, and many may even become self-sufficient. This trend can help many individuals and families become more wealthy. Based on the First Law of Wealth states, wealth goes up when the expenses go down.

Of course, basic needs are not the only expenses that will lower your wealth score. But some people find that they can accumulate surplus wealth over time that they will not spend because they reached their level of satisfaction.

THE FIRST LAW OF WEALTH IN ACTION

How does one progress from the state of being a consumer to then being an investor, and later to producing wealth for others? The beginning of wealth creation is the creation of a monetary surplus, and from a surplus, various investment possibilities will emerge. It will be necessary to evaluate these investment opportunities in a systematic fashion to decide whether or not to acquire any given asset. One of the first assets that many sophisticated investors acquire is an individual small business. The next chapter will explain how one can create real wealth from surpluses rather than designating the principal for consumption.

Who is wealthier: an average investor with a hundred thousand dollars in cash or a sophisticated investor with the same amount of money? It is a sophisticated investor because he has experience in utilizing the funds to create a monthly passive income. On top of that, he can increase his cash flow position. The sophisticated investor will not spend a large portion of the one hundred thousand dollars on repairing his present financial chaos or buying a more expensive car but will be able to invest the majority of his newly acquired funds toward investing in income-producing assets.

His wealth is determined by his ability to acquire new assets without sacrificing his capabilities to cover his expenditures. This ability is a combination of his financial resources, technical acumen, social capital, and education.

So, the wealth owned by different people has a different value. What do I mean by that? There is a component of wealth that comes from the ability to create periodical income from the assets. That is why wealth must have another inherent part, which is income.

Let's say, Tim, an ordinary thirty-five-year-old employee, wins one million dollars in the lottery. He can put the money in a bank and receive interest, which is a form of income—passive income. But that does not even cover the inflation rate. Tim is very cautious, and he does not want to spend all his money immediately. Tim wants to benefit from his new wealth without spending too much of it. He will need to think of a way to benefit from that wealth without selling it all off. Let's recall the First Law for Wealth:

Wealth = Passive Income / (Personal Expenses + Passive Income)

$$W = P / (P + E)$$

First, Tim put the full amount of one million dollars in his savings account. Tim plans to buy a nice home for half a million and use the rest of the one million to pay off his credit card debt and pay for his future personal expenses of about 3,000 dollars a month for about three years. But then he thinks, in three years, what will I do then? He will have spent all his money, and he will need to go to work again. By plugging in the number of this scenario into the wealth formula, he sees his wealth is zero:

$$W = P / (P + E) = 0\$ / (3,000\$ + \$0) = 0.$$

Tim changes his mind, and now he considers taking half of his million dollars to buy a positive cash-flow business with some employees or a great four-plex that he rents out. His new strategy would provide him with 4,000 dollars in passive income every month to cover his 3,000 dollars of expenses. He could still buy the same nice home in cash and have a great paycheck from his business or real estate to cover his expenses for a lifetime. Then his wealth is:

$$W = P / (P + E) = 4,000\$ / (4,000\$ + 3,000\$) = 0.57.$$

His score for wealth is higher than 0.5, and he would find himself in one of the upper boxes in the diagram representing the high wealth investors.

The example of Tim's decision is why I define wealth as a score that ranges from 0 to 1. Wealth has to do with the overall leverage you have in life given your expsenses and your income.

WEALTH VERSUS NET WORTH

I suggest you never confuse *wealth* with *net worth*. Net worth is all your assets minus all your liabilities. When looking only at your net worth, you could be deceived. Net worth does not tell you anything about your independence in the long-run and how you create your income. Also, it would help if you considered that wealthy people try to minimize their income to save taxes, which I will explain later in more detail.

THE SECOND LAW OF WEALTH: INDEPENDENCE

Being financially free is most important for every investor and, as a matter of fact, for everybody. The most precious resource of your life is your own time, and that is what you are getting with financial independence. The formula for financial independence is as follows:

$$Independence = \frac{Passive Income}{Salary + Passive Income}$$

$$Independence = \frac{P}{S + P}$$

The Independence Score is also a number that ranges from 0 to 1. The formula indicates that as soon as you take on a job and receive a salary, your wealth score is going down. Even if you do not need a salary to cover your expenses, taking a paycheck means you are sacrificing your time, and you are possibly paying avoidable opportunity costs. Steve Jobs did not take a salary when he joined Apple in 1997 as CEO. He was one of many one-dollar salary CEOs. Every CEO might have a different reason why they decided to take a salary of one dollar a year. But independence might be the biggest reason.

Your Independence Score should never be much lower than 1 (100%) to survive a soon coming revolution that is said to take millions of jobs. When artificial intelligence is threatening your job, unemployment support might help you out for a while. However, an Independence Score much lower than one makes you vulnerable because you might still need a paid job to cover your expenses. The time you spend working for someone else might be a lot of fun, and you might even learn from it. But when artificial intelligence is starting to take over your job, you wished you had spent some time to find out how to generate money differently.

WHAT IF YOUR PASSIVE INCOME IS NEGATIVE?

Believe it or not, many people buy assets, especially real estate, as an investment property that cost them money every month. Early in my career as an investor, I bought a beautiful little condo in an up and coming town. It seemed to be an excellent investment. The only problem was that I had to pay money every month to keep it. My passive income was negative. With my good salary, I was able to compensate for the negative passive income so that I could hold that asset. However, I needed to make my asset cash flow positive. That is where my journey started. I needed to get smarter about investing in more asset classes, and I began to get smarter about my cash flow and other asset classes.

SUMMARY: THE TWO LAWS OF WEALTH

I designed the *Two Laws of Wealth* to assess our financial situation using one single number. The numeric score ranges from 0 to 1, whereas the ideal score for Wealth and Independence is 1. A score of 1 is achievable for Independence by just not working for money.

However, it is far more challenging to achieve a score of 1 for Wealth unless you live on a remote island where everything is available for free, so you have no personal expenses.

Communism was an attempt to reach a Wealth Score of 1 for every citizen. However, this goal was never achieved because people's passive income was mostly government-supported and did not have any real value. People longed for products from the "West" and started smuggling goods on the black market to increase their *"real"* Wealth.

The Wealth and Independence Score only consider income and expenses and do not include the assets column, which can be expressed by the *net worth*. It is the value of all non-financial and financial assets owned by a person or organization minus the value of its outstanding liabilities. I suggest using net worth, Wealth Score, and Independence Score together to measure your financial situation.

PART THREE

MONEY

CHAPTER 12

Passive Income

"Stay hungry, stay foolish!"—Steve Jobs

Let us shed some light on how we create our income. If all of our money comes from our salary or wages, we spend most of your time and energy working for other people's business ideas. The pay is called income from active work, and since our time is limited, our income is not scalable. Active income is income that requires and is directly proportional to the expenditure of your own time and talents. If human beings had infinite time at their disposal and no physical requirements imposed on active labor, getting wealthy would mean always working harder. But that is not the case. Exhaustion and the sheer limits of time impose fundamental barriers to what unaided human labor can accomplish.

To become more independent, we will have to look for ways to receive recurring payments without contributing our time and effort. Making money, not as an employee or contractor, is called passive income. The Internal Revenue Service (IRS) defines that passive income can come from two sources: rental property or a business in which we do not actively participate, such as royalties from books or stock dividends.

The term passive income has now been discussed and proposed by countless sources for years. But why do so many people still do not receive significant passive income, and why is passive income becoming a must-have very soon?

Before we can receive passive income, we need to create or purchase the underlying income-producing assets. Most people are not trained or experienced in how to develop or acquire such assets. This is why I designed the following chapters to explain how to create such financial vehicles.

Here are some examples of financial assets that can create passive income:

- Rental income generated from real estate
- Dividends from preferred stock
- Companies that you own but are not managed by you
- Companies in which you have a share as a venture capitalist
- Interest received from loans you give to companies

WHY DO WE ALL NEED PASSIVE INCOME SOON?

In 2020, Hilton Hotels made 8.9 billion dollars with 169,000 employees, whereas newcomer Airbnb, a direct competitor, produced 2.6 billion dollars in revenue, with only 6,300 employees. These numbers not only reveal that the average employee at Hilton makes around $52, 000 a year, whereas Airbnb employees make a whopping $412,000 a year. But, what's more shocking, is that due to ever-improving technology and artificial intelligence, companies will need viewer and viewer employees to generate comparable or even *fewer* higher revenues. My prediction is that this trend will continue and eliminate most skilled labor jobs in the near future.

YOUR ASSETS AND YOU

The goal of all your financial investigations and decisions is to reach the point where your assets become a separate entity from your person, which you then can pass on to a new generation. You will be approaching that point when you are no longer dependent upon your active income to survive. If your passive income provides you with the ability to cover your essential needs, you are, in my definition, a sophisticated investor, and you will be able to build wealth for generations.

THREE TYPES OF INCOME

It is crucial to understand that there are very different tax laws for active and passive income. The IRS considers three types of income:

- *Earned* income
- *Portfolio* income
- *Passive* income

Figure 12.1 Three Main Types of Income (Graphic)

All three types of income differ greatly in their tax consequences. To find out more about income taxation, you can use the following table as provided by the IRS at www.irs.gov/taxtopics:

Income Type	Tax Code

Wages, Salaries and Tips	Topic 401
Interest Received	Topic 403
Dividends	Topic 404
Business Income	Topic 407
Capital Gains and Losses	Topic 409
Pensions and Annuities	Topic 410
Pensions – The General Rule and the Simplified Method	Topic 411
Lump–Sum Distributions	Topic 412
Rollovers from Retirement Plans	Topic 413
Rental Income and Expenses	Topic 414
Renting Residential and Vacation Property	Topic 415
Farming and Fishing Income	Topic 416
Earnings for Clergy	Topic 417
Unemployment Compensation	Topic 418
Gambling Income and Losses	Topic 419
Bartering Income	Topic 420
Scholarship and Fellowship Grants	Topic 421
Social Security and Equivalent Railroad Retirement Benefits	Topic 423
401(k) Plans	Topic 424
Passive Activities – Losses and Credits	Topic 425
Stock Options	Topic 427
Traders in Securities (Information for Form 1040 Filers)	Topic 429
Exchange of Policyholder Interest for Stock	Topic 430
Canceled Debt – Is it Income or Not?	Topic 431

Figure 12.2 *Types of Income and their Tax Codes*
(Source: http://www.irs.gov)

If you study the tax code, you will quickly find out that it is written for the sophisticated investor, as they will get the best tax breaks. However, these tax breaks are written primarily for businesses and not for individuals. We often criticize famous and public figures for not paying their fair share on taxes. This criticism is based on the fact *rich* people legally write off many of their personal expenses as business expenses through one or more of their companies. Then, they allow themselves a minimal salary to minimize their personal tax exposure, so their individual income tax can be reduced to almost nothing. With a rising number of sophisticated investors, this seemingly unfair practice can lead to less income tax collection for the government, a complex subject and it should be the subject of a separate book.

To summarize, being a sophisticated investor means your investor sophistication is comparable to a level 5 or 6 investors. Becoming a level 5 or 6 investor is a lengthy process that you can find more about in section Investor Levels earlier in the book. Although this book will prepare you for becoming a sophisticated investor, a considerable effort from your side is required to think and act like a sophisticated investor. If you look at the above table, you will get an impression of the type of assets that sophisticated or passive investors can buy.

CHAPTER 13

Starting a Business

"People, process and product." —Marcus Lemonis

Out of all five asset classes, businesses have by far the highest potential for providing the owners and all shareholders with the most significant returns.

I am dedicating this whole chapter on businesses because starting and operating a business today is easier than ever. The reason why it is easier is technology. Tasks from registering the company, creating a product or service, marketing, invoicing, and logistics are all supported by sophisticated software that is increasingly driven by artificial intelligence. You don't need to hire an armada of employees to run an entire online retail store.

I have talked to many people who shared with me their great business ideas, and only maybe a handful of these people have been able to create very successful businesses. Today, I am well aware of the reason for this small number of successes: having a great business idea may be a matter of days or weeks. Envisioning opportunities is easy. However, turning that vision into reality is the real challenge, and it will take months, if not years, to convert an idea into a successful business. Being not able to implement a great business idea is why many entrepreneurs fail, not lacking ideas. Some say nine out of ten start-ups fail within the first five years. My conclusion is: companies that can execute will succeed.

TURNING A VISION INTO REALITY

Before you start a business, you a clear vision of your company's purpose. Starting a business without the "why" is the biggest mistake that entrepreneurs make. In 1997, Jeff Bezos' vision was to create an online platform where people can buy *everything*. He founded Amazon, and his first mission was to sell books online. Later, he expanded to other products, and Amazon is now the largest online retailer globally. He followed *Simon Simon's* principle of "Start with the Why."

Turning a vision into reality requires the entrepreneur to play on all manuals. The key is that, before we can create any product or service, we need to create a machine that makes all products. When I started my first company, I often found myself in a vicious cycle that became unmanageable. For example, I could not find a developer to work on the product because I could not pay a salary. I could not pay compensation because I did not have any funding (except for my limited internal financing) or a paying customer. I could not bring in other people to work with me on the idea because I did not have a profit-sharing contract set up with a lawyer to offer potential partners or employees. The list seemed to become longer and more complex every day. I started to track all activities in a project plan and tried to prioritize all activities. I found myself doing classic project management, and I realized that creating a business is about managing a massive project. The good news was that managing all these project-like tasks is rather mechanical than really difficult, which meant that I could learn it. I learned how to deal with legal issues like copyrights, trademarks, and company profit-sharing contracts. I got knowledgeable about ways to search for investors and developers, and I created a team that will execute the first minimal viable product. I could build this product with the existing resources to develop the primary revenue stream.

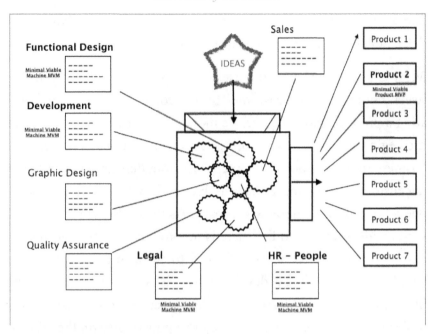

Figure 13.1 An example illustration for a business start-up machine.

In the end, I created a complete, well-oiled machine that will make all the products I would like to sell in a reasonable timeframe. I always try to build the machine in a way that allows me to scale the business, so I can, for example, add more products, include more sales channels, or increase the quality of the products.

Machine Part	Typical Management Activities
Legal	Create and manage patents, trademarks and copyrights
Marketing	Build and execute a marketing and business plan
Development	Generate business requirement documentation and technical specs, develop product, develop and implement company processes
Graphic Design	Create graphical design document and design products
Functional Design	Create functional design document
Sales	Create a sales plan, build sales channels and sign contracts with customers
Quality	Build quality plan and implement quality assurance (inspections, etc.)

Figure 13.2 Examples of areas a Business Owner has to manage.

The above table shows a sample list of management activities and deliverables in every area of a start-up machine.

Most entrepreneurs find themselves trapped in a vicious cycle between finding the first customer, having adequate funding, and creating a product that can generate money. The only thing available at the beginning of most start-ups is a vision and a business idea. The business engine cannot start-up until the founders have found a paying customer or created a first sell-able product or have found someone who will fund the new company. As illustrated above, it starts with an idea in the middle. There is no product, no funding, and no customer yet. The founders will need to work initially with many people until they find a developer who is willing to work on the first product. Or until an investor who agrees to fund the company's projects or a first customer is found, who puts money on the table to receive the first product. Eventually, the customer-product-funding machine will start running, and the owners can reinvest in more and better products, which will create more customers.

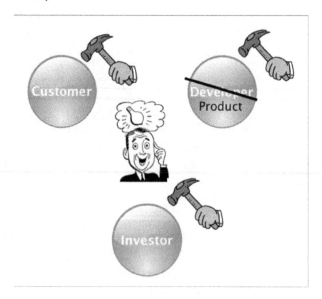

Figure: 13.3 The vicious cycle between finding a customer, finding an investor and creating a valuable and unique product.

To start an engine that draws attention to investors, creates products, customers, and money it can take a lot of energy and time. The entrepreneur will have to run around and talk to potential customers, investors, and developers who can make the first product. Entrepreneurs will need to knock on people's doors until finally, one will work with them. Many businesses fail due to the lack of either a customer, investor, or the right product. But when at least:

- *one investor* is willing to invest in an idea,
- *one customer* is willing to buy the first product, or
- *one valuable and unique product or service* is market-ready,

then, a business can be successful.

BUYING VERSUS STARTING A NEW BUSINESS

As an entrepreneur, you do not always need to start your own company. Many successful entrepreneurs have purchased an existing business that they have transformed over the years to become a different company. Or people have bought a profitable small business, which will create enough cash flow to fund a new company.

Here are some examples of successful business acquisitions: in 1979, Theo Albrecht, of Aldi Nord, bought Trader Joe's. In 1987, the original owners sold the Starbucks chain to former employee Howard Schultz. In 1951, Robert Maxwell, who founded the Maxwell Publishing Group, in 1951 purchased Permagon Press Limited, a minor textbook publishing company. He quickly built Permagon into a major publishing house.

If you are interested in more stories and biographies of the most celebrated entrepreneurs, you can find an excellent compilation of many entrepreneurs at *www.topbusinessentrepreneurs.com.*

When you buy a business, you generally buy at three main ingredients of a successful business: the products, the processes, and the people. Your purchasing contract should also clarify whether you buy any other assets like copyrights, trademarks, securities, or any other asset class like real estate or even commodities. You want to acquire hard assets like the machinery necessary to build the products, and you want to buy rights to sell to customers who have ordered at that business for years. With the customers and the products, you can generate income from day one after your purchase, and you can increase operations, quality, and customer base as you wish.

The disadvantage of buying a business is that you have to deal with its legacy, mainly existing infrastructure, which can hinder you from developing your vision. For example, when my partner and I purchased a printing and graphic design business in 2013, we spent many years to remove old equipment and inventory that was no longer usable. If you do it right, buying an existing company can provide you with the necessary funds to invest in other assets.

NOW, IT'S YOUR TURN!

What companies can you start? What companies would you buy? Would you like to convert a small business to a large enterprise? Look at your career experience and skills. You will discover that your background is the perfect mix to find customers for a product that you can develop, build, and sell. And, if you like to check out some cool business ideas, you can visit *ideasAI.net* and find out which real-life and in-demand business idea artificial intelligence GPT-3 suggests.

CHAPTER 14

Wealth Management

Wealth is Leverage!

I remember when people were sitting in their offices with huge newspaper pages and reports opened on their desks so they could study the latest financial news. There was no Internet or computer available.

Today, most sophisticated investors use the Internet and new technologies like blockchain to make their investment decisions and manage assets more comfortably based on real-time data. Gathering and pulling up data from the Internet is great, but how can financial asset management tools help?

With a financial asset management tool, an investor takes advantage of today's technology, especially mobile applications, to control all their financial assets. The most effective and crucial method to stay in control of your assets is to monitor asset income and asset value continually. Even in today's advanced world, this can still be a lot of work, especially if you own many different assets in different asset classes.

Many websites and services available on the Internet allow you to look up most financial data for free. However, it is still cumbersome to gather all the data regularly. I envision a tool that could do all the legwork for me by offering a dynamic, flexible, but efficient view of my financial assets. This tool could help me stay informed about all my investments and make better decisions.

As an investor, I promised myself that I would never again lose sight of the net income and the net asset value of all my financial assets. For that reason, I have developed a method to create a comprehensive view. Here is how it works using an example of Amazon Inc.:

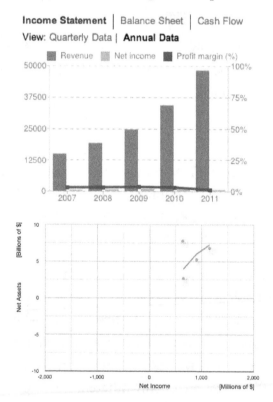

Figure 14.1 Amazon Inc. Income and Asset Value

The two figures show Amazon Inc.'s Net Income, Total Debt, and Total Assets. Based on these three numbers, a single view is being displayed automatically for each of my assets.

Whenever such a view is generated, the application will take a snapshot of these numbers and store them in the asset history. By plugging in the data from Amazon's income statement and balance sheet, as shown in the Asset Quadrants, you will see that Amazon has delivered financial results exclusively in the upper right cash cow quadrant. I will explain more about the quadrants and the meaning of them in the next section. It is essential now to realize that, if you create the Asset Quadrant diagram for NYSE companies, the dots would appear for most companies most of the time in the cash cow quadrant. The Asset Quadrants provide the investor with a quick view of the financial performance of a company.

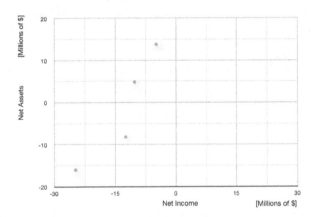

Figure 14.2 Cubic Energy, Inc. Asset Quadrants

I am showing another example of a company with very different financial results. In the four years shown, Cubic Energy, Inc. has produced only negative net income, and most of the time, their assets were less than their liabilities. They appear to be portfolio dead cows.

The net asset value varies hugely from industry to industry. So, a negative net asset or equity (assets are smaller than liabilities) might be considered acceptable in industries where big projects are frequent and extreme amounts of capital are needed. So, for a while, a negative net asset is deemed to be OK for some companies. However, if the asset imbalance seems to remain negative, you should not buy into such companies unless you are an excellent industry insider.

Now, you can analyze any company with this method and application. However, the most beneficial way to use this tool is by analyzing your assets. The same rules that apply to a for-profit company should apply to your assets. You want to grow them and want to receive a good income with your investments, correct?

This information will mean the world for you if you track your financial assets and act on the data. Income and asset value are the two only numbers that will determine if your assets are giving you your financial freedom or not.

So, let us look at the two diagram axis a bit closer: the horizontal axis is the income axis, and the vertical axis shows the value of the asset. Here is how the method calculates the numbers for both axes:

$$\textit{Income }_{Net} = \text{Revenue }_{Gross} - \text{Cost of Goods Sold} - \text{Expenses }_{\text{All Asset Related}}$$

$$\textit{Asset Value }_{Net} = \text{Asset }_{\text{Market Value}} - \text{Remaining Debt }_{\text{Asset Related}}$$

The gross income is the sum of all income that you receive from the asset in a specific time frame (e.g., a month). The revenue could be the rent you collect from a condo or the dividends you receive from your stock investments. The total expenses are all expenses related to that asset, including taxes. Depending on the asset class, these expenses might be account fees, property maintenance costs, loan service payments, etc.

The market value of your asset is the current money you could receive when you sell the asset. In the case of securities like stocks or bonds, you can quickly find its value on diverse online trading platforms, which reflect the current price on a public exchange system. In the case of real estate or business assets, finding a current value might be more challenging.

The total amount of loans related to an asset is the sum of all liabilities that we took when we bought the asset. It might be one or more bank loans, or it could also be an amount from internal financing. When we only used our own money to buy an asset, internal financing is 100%, and the leverage is 0%. If we bought an asset with a 10% down payment using our own money and used a bank loan for the remaining 90% to buy an asset, we used 10% internal financing and 90% external financing (leveraged with a bank loan). The asset is 90% leveraged. Important to note is also the total financing consists of internal and external financing:

$$Financing_{Total} = Financing_{Internal} + Financing_{External}$$

EXTERNAL AND INTERNAL FINANCING

External financing is when the investment money comes from a bank or another external source, such as external investors who need to be paid back. Internal financing is when the investor owns liquid assets like cash in domestic or international currencies or precious metals readily available to pay for an investment.

Good investors have, most of the time, the ability to chose between internal and external financing. There are advantages to both options, which I will describe later in more detail.

The risk of external financing is that the investor can get into a dead cow situation, where the asset is underwater. The debt servicing costs are higher than the income the asset generates. Do we have to pay for our assets every month to keep them? I promised myself that I would never again want to be in a situation where I had to pay to keep my asset. In December 1998, I bought my first newly built condominium not only for twice the market price. I also signed up for a loan for an interest rate that was too high, and a low principal payback rate. For ten long years, I had to pay about 500 dollars from my hard-earned salary every month to satisfy the bank that loaned me the money for the condo. Finally, in 2011, I paid off the entire loan, and I now receive a small paycheck every month. Buying this condo was an excellent lesson for me.

Over these ten years, I improved my financial literacy; I developed a method to track all my financial assets to ensure I am not buying into a dead cow investment again. I also wanted to find out how to develop my assets, so they will all produce income in a foreseeable time.

CHAPTER 15

Asset Quadrants

"The individual investor should act consistently as an investor and not as a speculator. This means that he should be able to justify every purchase he makes and each price he pays by impersonal, objective reasoning that satisfies him that he is getting more than his money's worth for his purchase." —**Benjamin Graham**

Figure 15.1 The Asset Quadrants

Imagine a grid with four quadrants. Everything we ever invest in will show up in one or more of these four quadrants. On the vertical axis is the asset value, and on the horizontal axis is the income generated from that asset. Both can be either negative or positive. A negative income means we pay every month for the asset. A negative net asset value means we owe more on the asset than it is worth. There is no equity in that asset; the amount we owe to the bank or our internal funding partner is higher than what the asset will sell for. In that case, we cannot sell the asset without taking a loss.

Furthermore, if we pay more in debt services to the bank, than the asset generates net income, the asset is in the death zone. We have to pay to keep the asset, and we cannot sell it without a loss. This situation is a financial dilemma, a disaster for every investor, and it happens more often than we might think. That's why I call the lower left quadrant the dead cow quadrant. There is nothing we can do to bring the asset back to life unless we lower the financial burden on the asset by, for example, paying off a portion of the entire loan. If the asset is in the right lower corner, we make money with that asset, even though the net asset value is negative. If we owe the bank more than the asset is worth, we might want to hold on to the asset, keep the money each month, and increase the net asset value over time. Then we might even be able to sell the asset with a profit.

Quadrant	Strategy	Pictogram
Young Cow	Invest	
Cash Cow	Monitor & Control	
Old Cow	Re-Structure	
Dead Cow	Abandon or re-develop	

Figure 15.2 Investment Strategies

I could also explain the net asset with the debt-to-equity ratio, the D/E ratio. If this ratio is higher than one, the asset is worth less than the amount owed to lenders. A ratio smaller than one means the net asset value is higher than the debt associated with that asset. So, it has a positive net asset value. The graph below represents an example of financial data from the electronic company Siemens. The debt to equity ratio varies over time quite a bit.

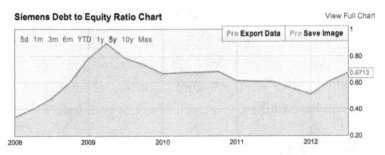

Figure 15.3 Source: http://ycharts.com/companies/SI/debt_equity_ratio

Now, in which quadrant would your like to be? In the upper right, correct? We can do a quick test by looking at the financial assets we own and make a dot for every asset based on the last financial statements we have. We will be surprised where you will find your dots. When I did my first asset diagrams, I noticed two things immediately: there were some in the dead cow quadrant, and most of them were in the young cow quadrant. I did the same job for some public companies like Siemens or Microsoft, and I saw a big difference. Both companies operated almost always in the cash flow quadrant and some times in the old cow quadrant. That opened my eyes immediately, and I started working on repositioning all my assets.

THE YOUNG COW

The young cow has not seen the world yet. It still needs much care; it is mostly inside the barn where it is protected and fed. A young cow is in an incubator and is waiting to be with the big cows to produce milk. We raise chickens in an incubator so that they can lay eggs. We do the same things with companies. We can find business incubators all over the country. The goal is to invest money in individual firms, so they become cash cows.

THE CASH COW

The cash cow has matured from a young cow into a cash cow. A cash cow does not fall from the sky. We have to create a cash cow. If you have proper financing (preferable internal funding), you will be able to buy a cash cow, and your asset will produce income from day one. If you leverage your asset, you might not receive immediate profit, and you will have to share your earnings with your lender.

THE OLD COW

Typically, a cow turns old after a long time of producing. Every asset needs continued maintenance and reinvestment. If these investments are too small or other market forces put too much pressure on an asset, your asset might still produce net income. However, the asset will lose in value so that it becomes an income-producing but underwater asset.

THE DEAD COW

The dead cow is the end stage of every asset. For businesses, the end-stage is bankruptcy or liquidation; for real estate, it is often a case of negative cash flow combined with negative equity. For securities and money market accounts, it is the devaluation of money combined with high fees and too little income from interest. There is typically no way out unless we can sell it to another investor with a more favorable financial restructuring.

HISTORICAL ASSET – VALUE GRID

It can be helpful to see income and asset value over time. Some assets move between all quadrants of the grid. One month they are cash cows, and other months they are dead cows. Sometimes you win, and other times you lose. Stocks are an excellent example of such a fluctuation. Most of the shares can move pretty fast on the value axis, and they can also provide considerable changes in the income they bring in as dividends.

It might help to use a tool that can create such a historical income-value grid. I envision a mobile application, which allows you to view real-time financial data on a grid-like display. The app would pull real-time information from global market places and combine them with your asset portfolio. It would create a grid for each asset that shows you how your asset is performing.

In the asset quadrants diagram, you can visualize the two dimensions of your assets: income and value. If you enter the current asset value and the monthly income from that asset into a table and build a scattered graph from that table, you will receive the asset quadrant diagram.

SUMMARY

The X-axis shows the income, and the Y-axis shows the current value of the asset minus all debt owed on the asset. You don't want to be in the left lower quadrant of the grid. It is the Dead Cow Quadrant. If you do not perform due diligence before you purchase an asset, chances are very high that you will end up in this corner pretty quickly. Even if the monthly numbers might vary and you are most of the time in any of the other quadrants, showing a red dot in the dead cow corner is a screaming alarm sign for every asset. And if you have leveraged that dead asset with a bank loan, you are trapped. You have to put out cash to sell it, and if you don't have that cash, your only option is to keep the asset and pay your monthly interest and principal. This situation is a typical underwater situation that many homeowners are in and even investment companies. Also, for many people, their house is their only significant financial commitment. So, not only do they have to pay the deficiency amount between their underwater home and the bank loan, but their house is also their only residence, so vacating it might be a substantial personal challenge. Later in the book, I will write more about your home as an asset.

A STRATEGY FOR EVERY QUADRANT

Depending on which quadrant your asset is in, you will need a particular strategy. The good thing is that there is always at least one appropriate strategy for all four quadrants. In the diagram below, there is a short hint about such an approach. The chart below shows a brief indication of what the investor faces financially in each quadrant. Your job is to control the investment process never to hit the "You lost" quadrant.

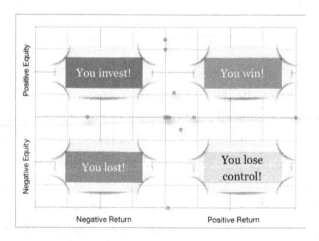

Figure 15.4 What happens in each quadrant?

CHAPTER 16

Ten Rules of Financial Sophistication

"Wealth is the Ultimate Business."

I have developed ten rules to remind myself to stick to my investment strategy. Of course, the list is not complete, but it is a start. Please feel free to add your own rules at the end of this chapter that you feel should be used to manage any of the five asset classes money, securities, commodities, real estate, and businesses.

1. NEVER BUY AN ASSET ABOVE MARKET PRICE

Buying an asset at or below market price seems obvious. However, I have seen too many times that investors end up paying too much for an asset. Warren Buffet says *"buy at a price at intrinsic value."* I started doing intensive research before I buy any asset, and I do my due diligence, which includes understanding the seller's motives to sell. Paying cash will always be an incentive for the seller to sell quicker.

2. FOCUS ON ASSETS THAT CREATE INCOME

By following only these first two rules, buying primarily assets that produce income for a reasonable market price can be a game-changer. You can minimize the investment risk and increase financial returns.

There are some exceptions, however. If the asset is a highly secure and liquid asset, which you can use to trade for other assets in the future, the immediate income may not be of importance. Some people say "cash is king" and "gold never gets old." So, instead of buying an income-producing asset today, it might be smarter to keep the cash or buy a non-producing asset to be able to obtain an income-producing asset later.

3. DO NOT KEEP DEAD COWS

Everybody who owned a Dead Cow asset like an underwater real estate property knows how dangerous a dead cow in a portfolio can be. That asset drains money continuously from the investor. Such an asset is worth less than I owe to the bank, and I have to pay every month to keep the asset. I will not even be able to sell the property without putting a lot of cash into it. So, I will never hold a dead cow. I will sell it, let it go, or pay it off, so I get it out of your liability column. Sophisticated investors never lose money!

4. NEVER OVER-LEVERAGE

When you leverage your investment, you should consider two questions:

- *First question:* is your annual income (annual return) from an asset you have purchased higher than the yearly rate you must pay for debt services related to this asset? You can read more about this principle in the chapter on liabilities and assets.
- *Second questions:* did you include a buffer to contain the remaining investment risk? You have often heard the advice: you should buy a condo in a good location, put down a small down payment, and take a bank loan to finance the rest. Many people suggest that it is wise to leverage as high as possible. That might work out great for your return on investment, of course.

However, you will take the full risk when the condo depreciates over time or your rental income decreases. Your loan payments might start to exceed the rental income, or the apartment might lose value and be worth less than you bought for.

5. MONTHLY ASSET STATEMENT

Create an asset statement every month showing income and current net asset value of all your assets.

6. STAY IN THE CASH COW QUADRANT

Aim to move all assets into the cash cow quadrant. It seems logical and even easy to accomplish. However, you can read it every day: businesses ran out of money, many real estate properties are in the red, and many money market accounts are just stumbling along, drawing money out of people's pockets. Concentrating on the cash cow quadrant can help to keep assets productive.

7. PUT YOUR ASSETS FIRST

If you lose sight of your assets, they can turn sour sooner or later. I recommend paying close attention to the financial performance of your investments. A safe and most successful investing method is to contribute money from your disposable income to specific assets weekly or monthly using automated transactions over a longer time. The accumulating value and the compounding interest from these investments can be significant. However, as a sophisticated investor, it is critical to be educated about the investment vehicle and align it with one's own strategic goals and expectations.

8. DON'T BE JUST A TRADER!

Do not trade your assets for capital gain purposes only. Trading is a profession and has little to do with investing. Think about the

2-bucket investing approach of level 5 and 6 investors. They make money by realizing their business ideas. They understand how to convert ideas into businesses and profits.

9. PUT INCOME BEFORE CAPITAL GAINS

Remove yourself from the community of speculators and return to the community of sophisticated investors. A regular and reliable income stream from all your assets should be your goal.

10. HAVE AN ASSET DEVELOPMENT STRATEGY

If you buy a young cow, you should have an excellent plan to develop it into a cash cow. Preferably, you can take personal control of the asset's development. If you purchase an old cow, you should create a concrete plan to convert it into a cash cow eventually. If you plan to buy a dead cow (underwater asset) from someone, you should structure the deal so that this new acquisition will be in the young cow or cash cow quadrant. And finally, you should always have at least a rough idea about how you plan to exit the investment. My general suggestion is to buy assets below the current market price and leverage as little as possible.

11. PLEASE ADD YOUR OWN RULES

_____

_____

_____

_____

_____

CHAPTER 17

Social Capital

Sophisticated Investors Work as a Team.

"If you work with people who aren't as good as you, then you become a country of midgets. If you work with people who are better than you, then you really grow."

—Steve Jobs

We might understand social capital as a measure of the value of relationships to people and groups we have and the impact that these relationships have on us.

If you want to become a sophisticated investor, you should invest in your social capital. Individuals on higher investor levels always work as a team; they have friends on higher investor levels that can help them with financial, legal, technical, business-related, tax, or other subject-specific questions. Sophisticated investors have a strong network of friends that mostly contribute to deals, business ideas, and businesses.

The average investor might have many friends, but not many are likely to talk about financial assets. If we want to improve our financial literacy and move up in the investor levels, we will need to build our network of people who are on higher investor levels.

Social media and online resources make it much easier today to find people in all areas. There are online and mobile systems like Meet-

Up.com, LinkedIn.com, and even messaging services like Twitter. com, which provide you with a wealth of opportunities to link up with like-minded people. For example, on MeetUp.com, you will find many groups that meet regularly in your town. There, you will find groups that talk about every one of the five asset classes. After you have identified groups you find interesting, join them, go to a meeting and talk to people face-to-face. You will find out quickly if you click with these people or not. If you feel misplaced in a meeting, you might try another group, or the subject you selected is maybe not for you. Try other groups until you find one that is for you.

Once you have found your group, meet regularly with your group, find out the people you can work with, and collaborate with them. Show them what you are working on, how you are currently investing, and ask questions.

It might take some time. But you will be able to come up with fresh business ideas, and if you do it right, you can soon collect income from your business to cover some or all of your expenses. At that point, you are free to explore more; you can put all your energy into developing your assets. Your journey as a sophisticated investor can begin.

The seven moral weaknesses are part of the old ethical codex, and their negative effect on society is taught for over 2,000 years. These weaknesses are pride, greed, lust, anger, excessive behavior, envy, and sloth. If you want to make good friends, especially in business, avoiding these negative traits will open many doors to you that were previously closed for you. Here are some simple lessons that I have learned during my entrepreneurial career. Don't be overexcited about your product. Don't become too focused on the money you are making on a product. Don't get carried away by your business friend's ideas, refrain from showing your anger overly, always be personal, don't send out mass emails. You should have role models, but you should only follow your own goals. In other words, be a friendly but firm guy. Be someone other people like to hang out with.

Some people say that *your network is your net worth*. So, build your social capital with caution and modesty. And always be of service to people. Believe it or not, being of service is the only real way to make money in the long run. Create a business with great people and create and provide things that people find useful and joyful. Of course, make sure you make money in the process. What does it help if everybody loves what you are selling but can't buy it anymore after being out of business?

CHAPTER 18

Asset Development

*Sophisticated investors not only buy financial assets;
they also develop their own.*

This chapter will explore what the life cycle of assets can look like and evaluate what investors can do to make sure their assets prosper.

Have you ever thought in detail about how and why your assets change over time, and how you can control them? A very effective way of following an asset's life path is by looking at the Asset-Quadrants.

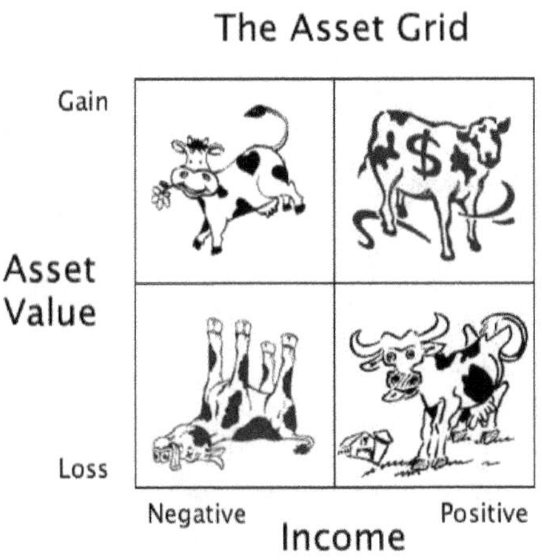

The Asset Grid

Figure 18.1 The Asset Quadrants

As explained in a previous chapter, this grid shows four quadrants: the young cow quadrant, the cash cow quadrant, the old cow quadrant, and the dead cow quadrant.

At any given time, assets will be in one of the four quadrants. Assets might even move from one quadrant to another quite often, triggered by certain events. We might not always be able to control how they move, but we will be glad we know that they have moved, so we can take measures to increase asset value and asset income.

When we buy an asset, we should know before purchasing which path we want our asset to move. Assets are born, fed, produce, are maintained, and eventually, they do die. Some investors will be able to give some assets a *second life*. But this will need a very high level of financial sophistication and very likely a great deal of cash.

ASSET DEVELOPMENT

Investors have to evaluate their assets continuously. The following pages illustrate how some typical financial assets can move from one asset quadrant to another. The value and income of these different types of investments change over time, and different wealth management strategies are required.

THE TRADER (THE MERCENARY)

The most straightforward asset development strategy is the most common and the oldest strategy: the investment in a non-income generating asset to sell it with a profit for a higher price in the future without adding any significant value to the investment itself, as illustrated below. This strategy was the prevalent way to make money during the Mercantilism period before the 17th century. Under this category fall collectors, traders, dealers, merchants, salesmen and -women, vendors, purveyors, peddlers, hawkers, merchandisers, distributors, suppliers, shopkeepers, retailers, wholesalers.

Figure 18.2 The Trader

THE FLIPPER

Some investors buy an income-generating asset, add value to it, and sell it with a profit. Many call it the 3-F's: Find, Fund, and Flip. The goal of this investment is to find an undervalued income-generating asset, fund it with usually higher leverage, and quickly resell it for profit after improving the asset. I illustrated this process in the below diagram. Typical investments using flipping are in real estate. Initial public offerings also fall sometimes into this category.

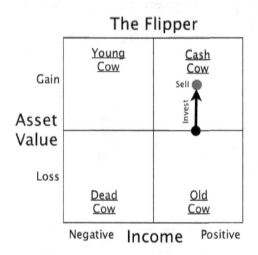

Figure 18.3 The Flipper

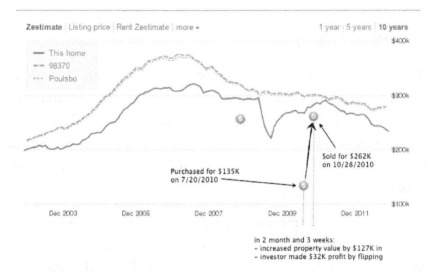

Figure: 18.4 Typical Real Estate Flip (source zillow.com, 8185 NE View Ridge Ln, WA 98370)

The above graph shows a real example of a real estate flip investment. A friend of mine presented this scenario during an event at the Real Estate Association of Puget Sound.

THE INCUBATOR (THE MISSIONARY)

An missionary investor puts money into an asset that is growing in value, brings the asset to operation to produce income, and then sells the asset after harvesting the income. An age-old old example of such investors is cattle farmers who raise cattle, generate revenue from selling milk, and after the typical life of a milk cow sell the older cow for slaughter.

Other typical such investors are people who start businesses with their initial capital and knowledge to sell the cash flow positive operative business with an often very large profit margin. There are many business incubators all around the country that provide young businesses office space, networking opportunities, knowledge, and other support during the start-up phase. Writing a book can also fall under the incubator investor.

Figure 18.5 The Incubator

THE BLUE CHIP INVESTOR

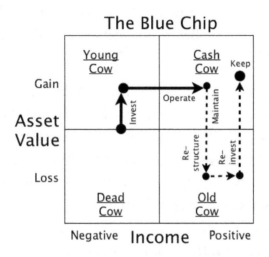

Figure 18.6 The Blue Chip Investor

Blue Chip investors are typically successful businesses that run well for decades. The business founders started small, increased the business value quickly, and became cash-flow positive sooner or later after inception. Proper management and suitable market climates helped the business to produce income over long periods. Management has recognized technological changes or social developments that could have caused the company to become obsolete, early. The company has remained a cash cow and has avoided turning into an old cow.

With the rapid success of electric cars, traditional car companies like Ford Motor Company or many German car companies will have missed the technological jump to the electrification of vehicles and are doomed to lose significant market share.

THE WISE INVESTOR

The wise investor sells an asset after growing it, harvesting the profits, and then loses the capability of maintaining, managing the asset. The asset becomes old. Before the asset stops producing income, the investor sells it.

I have seen too many times that the asset investor neglects many factors of investing, over-leveraging the asset, and then eventually ending up with negative cash flow. Often, the asset turns first into an old cow with a negative asset value, and then finally, the asset becomes a dead cow many times before the investor realizes it. At that point, the asset is over-leveraged, and it costs the owner money every month. Selling the asset is impossible unless the owner puts a lot of money down towards the deal. The asset becomes a liability literally.

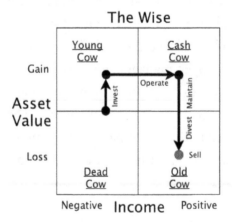

Figure 18.7 The Wise Investor

THE HOME OWNER

A frequent question I hear is whether a homeowner is an investor, or if buying a home is an investment. The short answer is: no. A longer answer is: it is a terrible investment. I show the asset quadrants for homeowners in this section because it explains the financial situation of every homeowner. The graph represents the only possible scenarios of homeownership. The final preferred outcome is that the homeowner owns the entire home without any debt owed to the bank after the mortgage is paid off. However, there will never be any scenario where the 'asset' (the house) produces any net income. Quite the opposite, the owner pays every month mortgage payment to the bank. And even after the homeowner has paid off the house, the owner will need to pay property taxes, utilities, and maintenance. For that reason, none of the dots will ever appear on the right side of the grid.

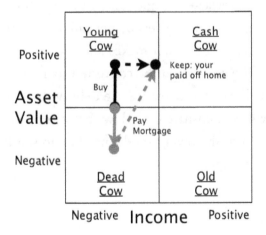

Figure 18.8 The Home Owner

THE NAIVE INVESTOR - A DEAD COW INVESTOR

Not all investors have enough experience to execute an investment strategy successfully. It all starts with the asset purchase. If the investor buys an asset for a price above the market value or the buyer over-leverages, the investor will end up with negative asset value. If the asset, on top of the negative value, does not produce any net income because the financial structure of the deal (e.g., too much leverage) was not evaluated carefully, the asset will end up in the lower-left corner the dead cow quadrant. The asset is underwater. Keeping it will require regular payments by the investor. The sale of the asset would result in a considerable loss and potentially an amount of deficiency needed to the loan company.

If an asset is worth less than the asset owner owes to a third party, it can become an old cow if it still produces income. After a re-evaluation of the asset, the asset is worth less than the asset's total debt. The owner cannot sell the asset without losing money. But since the asset is still generating income, the new owner can re-invest in the asset to increase its value. As a buyer, it makes a lot of sense to buy an asset as an old cow. The asset might be converted to a cash cow with the purchase if the buyer can refinance the debt with better conditions. Then, there will be a positive cash flow that can be re-invested into the asset. However, the owner might not like to sell it, as long the asset produces income.

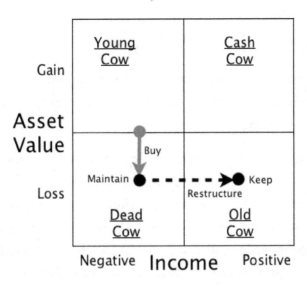

Figure 18.9 The Naive Investor

THE NEGLIGENT INVESTOR

Some investors buy and develop assets, make good money for a while, lose interest in the asset, have more important things to do, or get too old to manage the asset.

There are many examples of such a scenario. Many business owners who get older lose their energy to run their business. Another example is children who inherit assets from their parents but have not learned how to manage them—a typical case in which the wealth of generations is being lost. The critical moment of an asset is when the asset has already lost its value, and the income that it generates decreases. Once the asset hits the vertical axis and moves into the lower left quadrant, the asset is lost. It will fall into the hands of its creditors, who will only wait until the asset owner cannot pay the costs—like maintenance, fees, and loan payments that are associated with the asset.

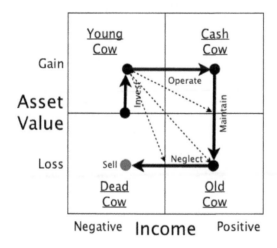

Figure 18.10 The Negligent Investor

THE LOSER

In case an investor makes the colossal mistake of paying too much money for an asset, the asset is underwater immediately after the purchase. Like dead stock in a store, it can't be sold on the market unless the seller takes a substantial financial loss. In case the asset is generating a negative return, as illustrated in the above diagram, the asset is a dead cow.

The diagram illustrates the sale of the asset as a dead cow. In the housing market, it is referred to as a short-sale, where the bank might share or ultimately pay for the deficiency between the sales price and the amount owed.

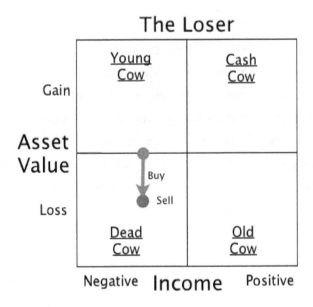

Figure 18.11 The Loser

FINAL THOUGHTS

Of course, the asset-income grid must be interpreted differently in different industries. Some industries, like construction companies, require high upfront investments and considerable leverage, and some do not require any debt to fund their projects and operations. This fact will affect the financial development of an asset significantly.

Furthermore, not all asset classes can be analyzed in the same way. For money market assets and securities, the income axis is not of great significance. Holdings in these asset classes are rather one-dimensional. People buy these assets to speculate that their values go up. Businesses and real estate are two-dimensional assets, meaning they vary in their net asset value (equity) and the income they produce.

As a general rule, assets in the dead cow quadrant are dangerous for you as an investor and need immediate attention. You can also find young cows, which should only temporarily draw money out of your pocket. You can use the asset quadrant diagram as general guidance. You should always perform your general due diligence before you buy an asset, and you should regularly analyze your assets' financial performance with different tools and methods.

CHAPTER 19

Unproductive Assets

"How in the world can I track my client's capital gains for Cost Basis Reporting?"—Quote from an Investment Broker in 2012

This book explains over and over that we should look for income when we buy assets. However, gold does not produce any income. Unproductive assets are not designed to generate income. So, why is it still worth owning some unproductive assets?

WHAT ARE UNPRODUCTIVE ASSETS?

Examples of unproductive assets are commodities like precious metals, cash, money in a non-interest bearing checking or savings account, any asset that you exclusively buy for speculation on capital gains, securities.

Typical Productive Asset	Typical Unproductive Asset
Bonds	Gold Bullion
Rental Properties	Cash at home
Savings Accounts	Consumer goods
Stocks with dividends	Stocks without dividend
Businesses	Checking Account
Cash Deposits (CDs)	Other Precious Metals

Figure 19.1 Typical productive and unproductive assets

Unproductive assets only move up or down in value. If we believe in pure two-dimensional investments, we should still consider holding some unproductive assets. These kinds of assets have their place in every investor's portfolio. Unproductive assets are like ammunition for a hunter. A hunter without ammunition, bullets for a gun, or an arrow for a bow, would be on a lost mission. Likewise, without liquid assets like cash or gold for internal financing, any investor will have a hard time buying a lucrative asset. Depending on our believes about how secure currencies are and how high we expect inflation to eat into your liquid assets, we can either increase our liquid assets with cash, gold, or other unproductive liquid assets. Their function is to act as a bridge, a sort of value custodian, while we are researching assets that will grant a return.

Cash is a non-productive asset. Money at home will not produce any income for you. Now, if you lend this cash to somebody and collect interest and principal over some time, then you have converted an unproductive asset into a productive asset.

This principle means we, as owners of an unproductive asset, can determine how we will use that asset. So, whether an asset is productive or not, depends primarily on the imagination of the investor.

UNPRODUCTIVE ASSETS AND TAXES

It is essential to realize that owning unproductive assets typically doesn't come without any costs. Examples of such expenses are storage costs, administration fees. Furthermore, the IRS has complex rules regarding capital gains and capital gains rates. As an investor, this means that maintaining a long-term or temporary position in unproductive assets can have hidden maintenance costs.

You should carefully balance and monitor the balance between the right number of productive and unproductive assets in your portfolio.

Remember: a productive asset, which does not produce current income, is called a non-performing productive asset.

I want to close this section with a quote from Warren Buffet, the chairman of Berkshire Hathaway. He is not a friend of unproductive assets, and in an interview on CNBC on May 7, 2012, he said,

> *"... when we took over Berkshire, Berkshire was selling at $15 a share and gold was selling at $20 an ounce. And gold is now $1600 and Berkshire is $120,000. but you take a broader example. if you buy an ounce of gold today and you hold it for 100 years, you can go to it every day and you could coo to it and fondle it and 100 years from now, you'll have one ounce of gold and it won't have done anything for you in between. You buy 100 acres of farmland, it will produce for you every year. You can buy more farmland, all kinds of things. And you still have 100 acres of farmland at the end of 100 years. You could buy the Dow Jones Industrial Average for 66 at the start of 1900. Gold was then $20. At the end, it was 11,400, but you would have gotten dividends for 100 years. So a decent productive asset will kill an unproductive asset."*

Earlier in 1998, he made the comment at a Harvard speech that *"[Gold] gets dug out of the ground in Africa, or someplace. Then we melt it down, dig another hole, bury it again and pay people to stand around guarding it. It has no utility. Anyone watching from Mars would be scratching their head."*

With all the negative words about unproductive assets, they do have an essential role for investors. They are a relatively safe place to put assets if no lucrative, productive asset is in sight; they are the ammunition that an investor can use to purchase productive assets. Recall that earlier in the book I talked about the two-bucket-principle, that explains how to pour cash produced by productive assets into the bucket of unproductive assets as storage of wealth, and then use this wealth to purchase more productive assets at a later time.

CHAPTER 20

Asset Acquisition

"The time of maximum pessimism is the best time to buy and the time of maximum optimism is the best time to sell."

—John Templeton

When we purchase an asset, the asset price is the most crucial factor when investing. However, several factors contribute to the success of the asset purchase:

- Purchase price
- Purchase time
- Market price
- Seller reputation and warranty
- Financing (internal or external)

Before you purchase an asset, you have ideally planned for your investment strategy and your asset development. You might desire to covert your asset from a young cow to a cash cow or from an old cow to a cash cow. If you pay too much, you may be instantly underwater, and if you leverage your asset too heavily, your debt service payments will be too high, so that your real returns will be negative.

With an over-leveraged asset purchase, you burden your portfolio, and it will draw money out of your pocket in the long run. However, if you buy a distressed asset that the current owner needs to sell, you might get an excellent deal, and you can buy it under its market value. If you keep the loan amount you take out to buy the asset low, the chances are that you will receive a good income from that asset.

You might have heard the saying: don't miss out on a crash! There is much truth to this statement. Most sophisticated investors can't wait to take advantage of an economic downturn, and they buy preferably after a significant market crash. This strategy works for dips of the entire economy and isolated market downturns like in the real estate market, the commodity market, or the securities market.

It might even pay off to look at the long economic cycle, which lasts based on Kondratieff for about 55 years. Being aware of significant past economic cycles might give you a hint on when to buy or sell. Important to note is also which asset classes you should buy in which cycle. You should purchase paper assets like securities and currency during the expansive cycle, and you should purchase tangible assets like businesses and real estate during the contractive period.

So, as a sophisticated investor, you learn when and how you will buy which type of assets. The general rule is to reinvest the money you receive from tangible, income-producing assets in other physical, income-producing assets.

CHAPTER 21

Bubbles and Schemes

"Long ago, Sir Isaac Newton gave us three laws of motion, which were the work of genius. But Sir Isaac's talents didn't extend to investing: He lost a bundle in the South Sea Bubble, explaining later, 'I can calculate the movement of the stars, but not the madness of men.' If he had not been traumatized by this loss, Sir Isaac might well have gone on to discover the Fourth Law of Motion: For investors as a whole, returns decrease as motion increases."

—Warren Buffett

Asset bubbles frequently happen in every asset class. Asset bubbles occur when asset values are inflated–when the market values are out of proportion compared to their real value.

There might be many reasons for asset bubbles to form. However, there are only two things of interest for an investor: "when is a bubble forming?" and "when will a bubble burst?".

Experienced investors have a generally good idea when bubbles start to grow. Often, they are even involved with the creation of the bubble. Smart investors pull out of the market before the bubble bursts, and everybody starts to panic.

Every investor will notice when a bubble has burst. But not every investor takes advantage of the situation; instead, many investors panic and sell everything they have. For sophisticated investors, however, this is the time when they buy assets. Sophisticated investors have learned how to control their fear and greed, and they are ready when others panic.

Asset bubbles frequently occur, sometimes intentionally created, sometimes just by a set of market forces, sometimes by a ship of fools heading in one direction, and one direction only. The general rule is to invest in an asset either well before the bubble starts to form or right after the burst of the bubble.

For example, it is obvious now that it would have been wise to buy real estate after the housing market collapsed in 2008 and 2009. Some properties, especially in California, have dropped in value by 50% within a few months.

BUBBLES VERSUS TRENDS

It isn't easy to know and see the difference between bubbles and trends. The general rule is: if there is a reasonable explanation of why a particular asset increases in value, then it is likely not a bubble.

THE GOLD BUBBLE

Investors often argue whether the gold market is in a bubble or if the gold price follows a trend. Why has gold risen from about 300 dollars around the year 2000 to about 1,700 dollars in 2012? So far, many gold investors seem to have a reasonable explanation for why the gold price is trending higher.

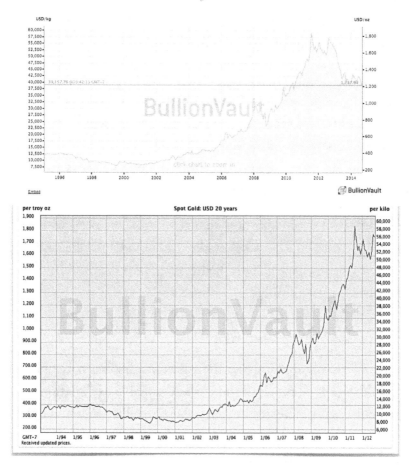

Figure 21.1 The Gold Price over between 1994 and 2014, BullionVault.com

STAGES OF A BUBBLE

It would be interesting to find out how the stages of a typical bubble can be detected. The stages of bubbles can be summarized as follows: stealth stage, awareness stage, mania stage, blow-off stage, and re-invest stage. I have been an investor in gold since 2004. In early 2013 the price was more than twice as high as in 2008. But, as with many bubbles, such assets often can be found in small markets and can easily be manipulated. So, a surge in demand can quickly increase demand, whereas a big sell-off tends to drop the price as fast. Prices are very responsive to irrational factors of emotions and popular press appeal.

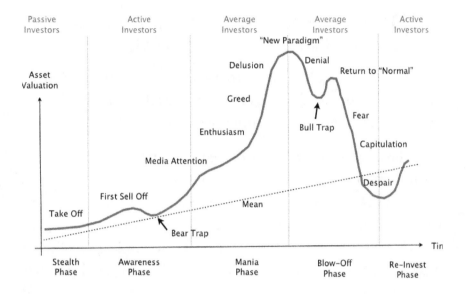

Figure 21.2 The stages of a financial bubble

Phase	Main Participants
Stealth	Passive Investors
Awareness	Sophisticated and Institutional Investors
Mania	Average Investor
Blow-Off	Average Investor
Re-Invest	Sophisticated and Institutional Investors

Figure 21.3 Main Stages in a financial bubble and their participants

THE SOUTH SEA BUBBLE

Did you know that Sir Isaac Newton lost almost his entire fortune of £20,000, which is the equivalent of about 300 million dollars in South Sea Company shares in today's money? The government and other interest groups hyped these shares in the early seventeen hundreds. He is known to have said, *"I can calculate the movement of the stars, but not the madness of men."*

LEGAL AND ILLEGAL PONZI SCHEMES AND OTHER FRAUDULENT INVESTMENT OPERATIONS

Large-scale systematic plans or arrangements to get something done or to put a particular idea into effect is how a scheme is defined. But there are good schemes and corrupt schemes.

A bubble is what occurs when a scheme that might have been successful in the beginning fails because too many people try to adopt it. Some interest groups might even create bubbles intentionally. This is true also for some business models for certain investment vehicles (financial products). They have a flaw, which is generally not detected by the vast majority of investors. These financial products are advertised to average investors, but there is no real value and tangible assets behind them, and the bubble grows with every new dollar invested.

One type of such a flawed investment vehicle is called a Ponzi scheme. Based on the U.S. Securities and Exchange Commission's (SEC) website, a Ponzi scheme is *"... an investment fraud that involves the payment of purported [false] returns to existing investors from funds contributed by new investors."*

It is a fraudulent investment operation that pays returns to its investors from their own money or the money paid by subsequent investors, rather than from profits earned by the individual or organization running the operation. Ponzi Schemes might be compared to the FIFO principle: *first-in-first-out.*

LEGAL PONZI SCHEMES

Legal Ponzi Schemes? It might not be very well known, but there are, in fact, legal Ponzi schemes. In general, as per definition, if an investment vehicle does not create any added value, it is likely a Ponzi scheme. Today, many claim that Social Security as it exists in the United States and many other countries today is one of the biggest Ponzi schemes of all time. Money from young people is deposited into a fund and paid to older people who had paid into the system when they were younger. Money from income-producing and economically efficient people is moved to the inefficient—a situation that I will explain later does not support the wealth of generations.

It can be argued that the stock market is also a giant Ponzi scheme if the current retirement system is based on 401(k) and IRA plans, which contain mostly stocks and equity funds. Money is poured from the currently employed people into a system that will pay the unemployed or retire.

Many argue that taxes and our government-run social security system are legal Ponzi schemes. Maybe it is time to depart from these most inefficient economic systems and imagine solutions that will improve the economy by applying sophisticated investors' market rules instead of such schemes.

THE WORKINGS OF THE BANKING SYSTEM

The basis of our entire economy is, of course, a monetary system. All goods and services in America are sold primarily in dollar-denominated amounts. But where does our money come from? At the base of the pyramid is the Federal Reserve System's ability to issue Federal Reserve Notes. Now, what is a Federal Reserve Note? It is a piece of paper backed up not by a specific tangible value but rather by a promise, and the promise is not by the Federal Reserve

System but by the United States Government. Now, where do you see the promise on a Federal Reserve Note? The following language appears: 'this note is legal tender for all debts public and private.' Let us look carefully at the words of the promise. In plain language, it says it is legal to use a Federal Reserve Note to pay debts. But that is all it says. There is no mention that the note is backed up by the United States' full faith and credit. To get that added protection, the Federal Reserve Note must be transferred into a banking deposit in an FDIC insured bank. So, what is a Federal Reserve Note worth? It has not assigned value. It is a floating currency (or fiat currency), as are most currencies operating in the world markets today. To calculate its value, it is then necessary to consult the currency trading markets daily. What does all this mean for you as a holder of Federal Reserve Notes? It means that you are negotiating not a thing but a promise, and a variable one at that!

Now, most people think of money as a thing. But that is not what money is. Money is symbolized power. Money allows actions to continue in the real world. But the degree of the control can vary with markets, with timing, and as measured against other measures of money. This chapter deals with schemes. Well, the concept of banking is both a useful scheme and a mystical scheme. It is mystical because banks can use Federal Reserve Notes to create value out of nothing. Here is how they do it. The Fed has the power to issue banknotes to banks by only printing them. They have no inherent value beyond the ink and the paper. Their value is entirely dependent upon the money supply and the continued support of the United States government, which has given the Fed the power to print money. In the United States Constitution, the power to create money is granted only to the government. Question: is the Fed a government entity? The strict answer is no. The Fed's actual status is that it is a private corporation to which the Federal Government has licensed the ability to create money. Here is the significance of this: the Fed does not have to maintain a separate holding of gold to back up its currency. This means that there is no resource for the holders of Federal Reserve Notes in case of a national catastrophe.

In summary, our monetary system's security is based only on our faith in the financial system. In contrast, productive assets have proven in history to create wealth.

REVERSE SOCIAL SECURITY

Bubbles and Ponzi schemes will inevitably reach a point where they can no longer perform to the investors' expectations. Those expectations were excessive, to begin with, and based on an illusion. The illusion is similar to the dream of perpetual motion because there will always be friction to slow the machine down.

So, our current retirement system is built on the following assumptions:

- The benefits for the retirees are never exceeding the contributions by the young or the system would become a Ponzi scheme.
- The income of retirees is not only composed of their social security income but mostly on other retirement income sources since it was only designed to be a safety net.

So, most western nations have not designed the current retirement system to carry wealth from one generation to another. It has instead been designed as a fragile safety net. Can we create social wealth over time, so retirees become a capital source instead of draining it from the younger generations?

Absolutely! We could, for example, think about a Reverse Social Security System where older people contribute to the younger generations. How? Human progress has always depended upon the service of the young by the old. For example, where would science be today if inventors and researchers took their knowledge to the grave?

Capital should always increase so that we can finance human progress. I can only see this happen when we liberate the young from the skilled labor force and empower them to be part of human-centered capitalism.

Moral dilemma: the current zeitgeist teaches us to become rampant consumers. And consumerism benefits big business. This development has led our society into a lack of investor sophistication. But if people accumulate enough investor sophistication early in their lives, they will have more than enough financial leverage when they retire. Such retirees might desire and feel the moral obligation to support young people while the young generations can invest in their education, experience, and financial assets.

With a government or company backed retirement system, most people live in the illusion of false security instead of realizing that their financial and spiritual experience must secure the young as much as young generations offer older people's wellbeing. Let me explain the point that I am making here. The human life experience depends upon the passing on and the actual witnessing the actual stages of life. When people exist in age-segregated ghettos, the only people that they can learn from are people of a similar age. Such a situation means that they do not always have the skills to face the predictable life crises that lie before them.

CHAPTER 22

Dead Cows

"I swore I was going to exclusively collect assets and not liabilities for the rest of my life. I swore never to take gambles I couldn't back up, or that I couldn't afford to lose. And, I've stuck with that ever since."

—Tim Blixseth, real estate developer, record producer, songwriter and timber baron who is known for co-founding the Yellowstone Club in Montana

Yes, when you invest in assets, the chances are that at least one of your assets will become a dead cow. I am talking about an asset worth less than you purchased it for, combined with the fact that it produces a loss each month.

AN EXAMPLE

Assume you own a rental property in an up and coming town. It has always produced a high rental income each month and each year. But after some years the local rental market 'tanks,' you lose your tenant, and while you are trying to find a new tenant, you discover that your monthly return on that property has turned negative. The search for a new tenant combined with the lower monthly rent income has now caused a significant loss for the year. Even worse: due to the lower locked-in rent, the coming years will likely also be in the red.

To make matters worse, the housing market in the town where you bought the property also tanks considerably over the years. So, the money you owe to the bank is now more than what the property is worth. Now, this is a typical dead cow situation. What should you do with it? Do you sell it for under the price that you owe the bank? No, this would require you to put perhaps several thousand dollars on the table to pay the deficiency. Should you keep the property in the hopes that the rent goes up and the housing market will increase so that you can sell it with a profit? Well, that is the way most property owners handle such a situation. But both options are incredibly costly.

BEING UNDER WATER

An overwhelming number of homeowners are underwater. CoreLogic's latest figures from the research firm indicate that at the end of the last big recession in 2008, 11.1 million, or 22.8%, of all residential homes with a mortgage were underwater. Many investment firms own assets that are underwater also. For example, Behringer Harvard Holdings LLC, a real estate investment firm, dropped a bombshell on its clients at the end of 2012. It announced that one of its largest funds, one for wealthy and fully accredited investors, was underwater. The investment company Behringer Harvard Holdings took several loans to support their Strategic Opportunity Funds in hopes that they would rise in value. Huge loan payments were needed for banks and other business entities from which they had borrowed money.

I was personally in this situation for almost a decade with a condo that I purchased in 1998. Luckily, I was able to keep the property by paying the monthly interest and a low principal payment for these years. At the same time, I was able to save enough money to pay off the entire loan amount to the bank. After that, I even made a moderate profit with that rental every month. I managed to convert my dead cow into a cash cow. However, it is still worth less than what I paid for it.

MY FIRST ASSET WAS A DEAD COW

Let me explain here how I got myself into this unfortunate situation. After I graduated from college, I worked for a couple of years in the software industry, and I made my first good salary as an employee. Much of it I spent on personal traveling, on some cool gadgets, and on other small items that I can no longer remember or have long donated to charity.

In 1998, after about two years of working, a friend of a coworker approached me and said, "Why don't you invest in a beautiful condo in an up-and-coming town in East Germany and benefit from some of the advantageous government tax subsidies? Since I wanted to get into real estate at that time, I bought the property without much hesitation and with little due diligence. After I completed the deal, and after a few years had passed by and after doing some more extensive research, it turned out that I had paid twice the amount of what the property was worth.

I paid monthly about 500 dollars in loan services with a rental income of only 300 dollars. Moreover, the value of the property never reached even half of what I paid for it. And this has remained true to this very day.

Well, you might say I deserved nothing better since I did next to no due diligence before purchasing the condo. And you would be right. I had no experience in real estate at that period of my life. I was not even aware of the risk of losing money with this investment. It turned out that my investment was a dead cow from the very beginning. I owned an asset that costs me money every month, and an asset for I owed more money to the bank than the property was worth. It was indeed a bad investment. I had to pay both interest and principal to the bank every month, and I only got about half of those costs from the renter. The only positive was that I always did have a renter since the property is located in a popular downtown area in a mid-sized town in Germany.

Thirteen years later, I still owned this condo, and I managed to make it work. However, to convert it from a dead cow status, I needed to pay off the entire loan in one lump sum so that I owned it free and clear.

I recently learned that I was not the only one who made such a wrong investment choice. Others went through this same investment nightmare. Many famous Germans, including a well-known German TV talk show host and a national league soccer player, had invested in real estate properties from the same company around the same time as I did. They lost millions of dollars and had to declare bankruptcy. These examples show that even those we often think are financially sophisticated can also wind up with dead cows.

SO, HOW DO YOU GET RID OF A DEAD COW?

There are four basic exit strategies if you need to get rid of an asset that pulls money out of your pocket each month and is worth less than you still owe for it.

These are as follows:

OPTION I - KEEP THE ASSET AND MAKE THE PAYMENTS EVERY MONTH.

If you can afford option I, you should hold on to the asset if you believe that it can become a cash cow in the foreseeable future.

OPTION II - SELL THE ASSET AND PAY THE DEFICIENCY TO THE BANK.

If you can quickly sell the property on the open market and if it is not likely that the market value of similar assets will increase in the near term, you should do so.

OPTION III - PAY OFF THE ENTIRE LOAN OR PORTIONS OF IT TO BECOME CASH FLOW POSITIVE.

This option is the refinancing of the loan. May the interest rates have dropped since you received your initial loan, or you may have found other sources for better credit. If you still believe your money was well invested in the property because it can yield a positive cash flow after the loan re-payment, you might consider option III.

OPTION IV - ABANDON THE ASSET.

To some extent, it is a misnomer to refer to option IV as an option. Many people find themselves in a situation where bankruptcy is the only option. Declaring bankruptcy is the only choice for some. It will give a person or a company a second chance after making a particularly poor investment choice.

Another way to abandon an underwater asset is a strategic default. In short, this is when the borrower can convince the lender that they are not able to make the loan payments anymore, and the lender agrees to forgive them all remaining debt after selling the asset. For the bank, this option is a troublesome scenario, and you need to make sure you can sustain the results of a lower credit rating. I have personally seen some of my friends and business partners go through this process. I know how emotionally difficult this situation can be, especially when the money owed is for your residence.

Before you decide which of these four options work best, you should get detailed information from your bank regarding pay-off terms, principal modifications, and refinance options. You should inform yourself about the bankruptcy laws and consult a lawyer if necessary.

SUMMARY

#	Solution
I	Keep the asset and make payments every month
II	Sell the asset and pay the deficiency to the bank
III	Pay off the entire loan or portions of it to become cash flow positive
IV	Abandon the asset, declare bankruptcy

Figure 22.4 Exit Strategies from Dead Cow Assets

CHAPTER 23

Liabilities and Assets

"An asset is an investment that puts money in your pocket, a liability is an investment that takes money out of your pocket."

—Robert Kiyosaki

Using debt as leverage for investing is like handling fire. You will need to learn how to handle a flame without burning the whole place down. Debt is a financial tool. If you want to use it, you will need to learn how to handle it properly.

If for any business reason, you decide not to pay for the asset using your funds, you can choose to finance a portion or most of the purchase price of the asset by taking out a loan from a lender. That might be a brilliant idea if you can come up with a plan to make money even though you will now have to pay interest on the loan. Taking a loan to invest in an asset is called financial leveraging.

Business deals can be structured in many ways. Depending on the debt structure, the asset will produce net income, or perhaps it will not. When the loan you take out to purchase the asset is too large, this is called over-leveraging the asset. Over-leveraging means that the loan you take out to acquire the asset is too big and will result in squeezing the profit margin out of any income that the asset produces. Thus, you can end up with a monthly loss. Any time you do this, you have acquired a liability and not an asset because you are now losing money.

EXAMPLE OF EXTERNAL FINANCING: A CONDO-MINIUM

As an example, let us look at a potential purchase of a condominium. Suppose you want to purchase a condo and you have $30,000 of your own money to invest. Let us further assume you can buy a 2-bedroom condo for $80,000. You put $30,000 down and take a $50,000 bank loan with an 8% annual rate you will probably pay about $500 monthly for 15 years to service the debt. Let us assume further that you hope to receive rent payments of about $900 a month, and you allocate $100 a month for maintenance, vacancy, and property taxes. Your monthly income in this case would be $300 ($900 - $500 - $100 = $300). So, you will have about $300 leftover, which is your monthly net income based on your initially invested 30,000 dollars. That is an annual return of 3,600 dollars or almost 12% return on the money you initially invested. The formula would be:

Return on money invested = net income divided by money invested. Using this formula in the above calculation would yield the following figures: 3,600/30,000=0.12 or 12%

EXAMPLE FOR EXTERNAL FINANCING: TRUCK

Let's look at another example. Suppose you have an American Express business card limit of 30,000 dollars, and you use your credit card to buy a new pick-up truck for 20,000 dollars to support your delivery business. You plan to use the vehicle to deliver goods to your customers, and with the help of your new truck, you can increase your monthly business income by saying 10,000 dollars. So, you now spend monthly 2,000 dollars each month to pay the interest and principal on your American Express card to service the debt. You can now expect a net return of 8,000 dollars per month based on this financing decision. In five months, you will be debt-free. You were able to pay off the loan in a very short time, and you will have the truck for a useful period of perhaps four years at 25,000 miles per year. The new vehicle will help you to generate an additional income of 8,000 dollars per month.

So, applying our general formula, the return on your money invested is as follows:

Net income/money invested = (12 x $6,000) / $0 = infinite return.

The return in this scenario is infinite because the denominator is zero. So, let us look at what we have done in this instance. When you do not invest any of your own money, you leverage your investment 100% and hence receive an infinite return. All the money came from an outside source. So, it is possible to say that the return on your own money in this instance is infinite. It becomes clear that when a lender finances your entire asset, your financial gain is infinitive. As long as the asset produces more than you pay for the debt service, you can always make a profit.

You might wonder why not always leverage 100%. The answer is simple because banks typically don't lend the entire amount but require down payments or other collateral. However, the higher your investor level is, the more likely your lender will offer you a loan with high leverage.

INTERNAL FINANCING VERSUS EXTERNAL FI-NANCING

- In general, there are different benefits for internal as opposed to external financing. If you make a low down payment when purchasing an asset, your external leverage is high, and your internal leverage is very low. On the other hand, if you pay a lot of money towards your investment, you will only need to leverage the purchase with a small loan: your external leverage is low, and your internal leverage is high. Both a high internal and high external leverage have their benefits and drawbacks. The net income depends heavily on the amount that you leverage. Higher leverage requires higher debt payments and will lower your profit. As a general rule the following statement can be made:

- If the return on investment (ROI) is higher than the interest rate (APR) that the lender offers you, a higher external leverage will increase your return on your invested money.

- Whereas, if the return of your new investment was lower than the Annual Percentage Rate (APR) offered, you would decrease your return when increasing the leverage.

WHAT IS THE LEVERAGE INDICATOR?

So, how can you quickly determine whether you should take out a loan to leverage your proposed investment or not?

Here is a general formula that I recommend using to answer that question. I call it the *Leverage Indicator* or L:

Leverage is equal to the return on equity (ROE) divided by the annual percentage rate (APR):

$L = ROE / APR$

Please note that the return on equity (ROE) is not the same as the return on investment (ROI). ROI is the money that you receive as income from the entire asset. ROE is the money that you earn as income from the share of the asset in which you have an ownership interest, which is directly related to the money that you have personally invested initially.

Please note that your share of the new asset is a constant contrary to many beliefs. Namely, your percentage increases over time when you pay back the loan. When you take a loan, you do not own the asset and incur liabilities against the asset. The liabilities condition the asset.

So, in other words, ROE is compromised by the liabilities and certain usage conditions set by the lender and tied to the asset. The banker will tell us that our equity in an asset rises with the loan's gradual pay-off. However, we have to understand that our initial stake is the initial down payment that we invested. The interest and principal paid throughout the loan is the cost of the financing that we have decided to procure. The bank might consider increasing your credit as an opportunity to loan you more money. So, from their point of view, it is logical that they say your equity has increased when, in reality, the collateral backing up your loan has increased.

In this book, I try to make you thinking about how to evaluate the investment potential, and what it means to your cash flow when you finance your investments.

Let us look at a simplified example: you want to buy a condo for 80,000 dollars, which provides an annual net income from the rent after debt payments, taxes, and maintenance of 4,000 dollars. If you pay cash for the condo, your return on your money-invested (Return on Equity ROE) is 5% (4,000 dollars / 80,000 dollars). If the bank offers an annual interest rate APR of 6% to borrow money, then Li is 5% divided by 6%, which is 0.833, smaller than 1. If Li is smaller than 1, then ROI is lower than APR, and you should not get a loan to buy this condo (see scenario C below). Whereas if the net income were 8,000 dollars, your rate of return on equity would be 10%, then Li is 10% divided by 6%, which is 1.67, and that is a value higher than 1. You should take a loan to increase your leverage on this investment. The loan would increase your ROI when you increase the external leverage (see scenario A). The three following diagrams illustrate these three different scenarios: A, B, and C.

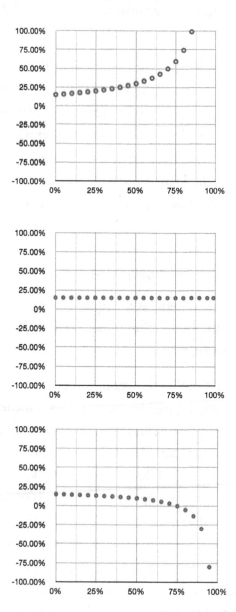

Figure 23.1 Leverage Indicator Scenarios A (top), B and C (bottom). The Y-axis illustrates the return, the X-axis shows the percentage of financing.

Return vs. Interest Rate	L_i	EXTERNAL LEVERAGE	Recommenda- tion
A: ROI > APR	>1	You will make more money the more you leverage externally	Leverage as high as you can tolerate.
B: ROI > APR	=1	No matter how much you leverage, your return will remain the same	Don't leverage the investment.
C: ROI < APR	<1	Every external lever- age will decrease your return	Don't leverage the investment.

Figure 23.2 Leverage Indicator Recommendations

In scenario **A, the ROI** is higher than the same investment with any potential loan. Scenario B is a theoretical case where the bank interest rate is exactly equal to the investment return. No matter how high the external leverage would be, the investor would always get the same return. And scenario C covers the case when the asset's performance is lower than the bank interest rate APR. In the case of C, taking a loan reduces the investment return when increasing external leverage. Only in the case of A, higher leverage will increase the return of the money invested. If you can fund an investment 100% with external funds (100% leverage), you will theoretically make infinite returns. Here is why: when you invest zero dollars any return you receive will be infinite due to the formula for return on equity (ROE):Return on Equity (ROE) [%] =

(Net Income / *Money Invested*) x 100

Money Invested is 0, and any number divided by zero is infinite.

WHAT IF I STILL WANT TO BUY BUT DON'T HAVE THE MONEY FOR IT?

Banks typically don't tell you whether you should take a loan or not. The bankers won't tell you about a Leverage Indicator. A bank most always wants to sell you a loan as long it works for the bank. But this does not necessarily mean that it will work for you. In almost all cases, the bank asks for collateral assets, which they can put a lien on when they give a loan.

Today in America, it seems that almost all home buyers take a bank loan to purchase their house. I want to point out that the Leverage Indicator Li with a home purchase is zero since the home generally doesn't create any investment return. Li = ROI / APR, and when ROI = 0 then Li is 0, too. But these home buyers still buy the properties because they want them. For an investor, this makes absolutely no sense. As you can see in the above figures, a 20% down payment and an 80% bank loan provide them a negative 25% ROI every year independently from the house's purchase price (annual loan payments divided by (property purchase price - mortgage amount).

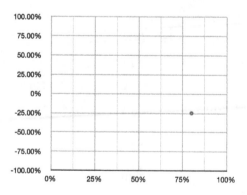

Figure 23.3 ROI of a Home Buyer is 0, Li<0

BUYING STOCKS ON MARGIN IN 1929

But not only homebuyers make these irrational investment decisions. Believe it or not, in the late 1920s, taking a bank loan to buy stocks was the hippest thing to do. Average investors, inexperienced investors, and even sophisticated investors started to buy common shares on the New York Stock Exchange market "on the margin" as it was called back then. The problem with that was that people were speculating on the stock price, and hence they were guessing the rate of return they would make when they finally sold the stock. Nobody knew where the price of a stock was going, so nobody knew the return rate (ROI). ROI was a huge variable number. The interest rate from the broker however, was given when they took the loan. The ROI was the big unknown. So, people didn't know if they bought into scenarios A, B, or C as illustrated in the grid diagrams before–it was indeed a big gamble. And as you can see in situation C, as soon as the return went below the interest rate, the return on their investments could turn negative very quickly even before the stock price went below the price when they purchased the stock.

As you might remember, it was the time of the Great Depression, and some argue that buying stocks on margin was one of the most significant factors that caused this economic turmoil.

THESE ARE THE TWO MOST IMPORTANT LESSONS I HAVE LEARNED FROM MY INVESTMENTS:

My first condo made a 3.3% rate of return on the purchase price. However, my bank loan was 6.2%. So, taking any credit to buy the condo was not a good idea in the first place. But it gets worse: since I was new to investing and the bank agent was an excellent salesman, I agreed to leverage the purchase with a 95% bank loan. As a result,

I paid a significant amount in interest and principal every month, which was higher than I collected in rent. Years later, I calculated that I needed to pay down at least 50% of the price of the condo only to break even. I finally did pay off the loan after ten years of carrying this dead cow along in my portfolio—doing simple math before the deal will determine the success or failure of your investments. Doing your due diligence makes the difference between owning a cash cow or a dead cow.

The above diagrams illustrate my situation very well: based on the leverage indicator formula Li, which was smaller than zero, I should have either negotiated the interest rate of 6.2% down to less than 3.3% or I should have paid more than 50% of the purchase price with cash.

CHAPTER SUMMARY

THE GENERAL RULE OF LEVERAGING:

If the return from your asset (return on equity) is higher than the interest rate you will pay for a bank loan, I recommend to can get a bank loan to buy your asset. If the return from your asset is lower or equal than the interest rate that you will pay for a bank loan, you should NOT get a loan to buy your asset.

Only leverage an investment with external money when:

- The rate of investment return is higher than the interest rate you pay to the bank.
- The rate of investment return is somewhat constant over time (like rent income from a condo or income from bonds)

GETTING A LOAN TO PURCHASE YOUR HOME IS GAMBLING!

In no case is it financially favorable to take out a loan to purchase your home. The mortgage rate you pay reflects a negative return, which is smaller than the interest rate you pay to the bank. If you intend to sell your house with a profit some years later, you might get a return due to a general housing market increase. The total growth might then be higher than the sum of all mortgage payments you made, but it is still a dangerous proposition you are in since you are nowhere in control of the housing market.

Here is how I would describe my journey to investing: as a young person, I started creating nothing out of nothing, as I did with my first condo. As I grew older, I started getting a little bit of something out of nothing but most everything else I had to work hard for. Now, I try to build something with my mind and morals, using my skills, habits, social network, and intuition. My point is that I can leverage my experience, and others trust me to do so. I can invest in more assets with less of my own money.

My book's message is that wealthy people can create something out of nothing, and poor people have to pay the full cost of leveraging everything. Sophisticated investors are increasingly able to find people to trust them, which decreases their costs of credit while also increasing the amount available. This situation lets them do big things.

CHAPTER 24

Exit Strategies

*Try to eliminate any relation between
your income and the amount of hours you work.*

Before you buy an asset, you need to plan how to exit the investment after owning and maintaining your asset. In my experience, not having an exit strategy is the number one mistake that investors make. You always need an exit strategy, even if you plan to hold the asset forever. Then your exit strategy is not to sell the asset and collect income from it. The exit strategy is one of the first strategies when planning the asset development, even before you purchase the asset. Not having a strategy has left many investors with significant losses.

However, the most challenging part when buying, developing, and exiting an asset is managing your emotions. Many investors get attached to their assets, and parting from them or restructuring them does not always seem to be as easy as one would think.

Before you buy and as long as you own the asset, you will need to answer the questions when and how you will sell or restructure your asset. It would help if you always looked out for other investors who you can sell your asset to. Even if you buy an asset purely for income generation and intend to keep the asset, I recommend always considering offers you receive for your asset and regularly researching the market for your asset. Being a sophisticated investor means that you continuously have control over your assets. And that means that you always have an answer to any question someone would ask you about your investment– especially when it could lead to selling it.

As follows are typical exit strategies that every investor should consider before putting money into any asset. It is crucial to pick the asset strategy and then elaborate on your approach after the purchase. This tactic will increase your ability to plan, and it will lower your investment risks.

Investment Strategy	Trigger Event	Description and Examples	Typical Techniques and Skills
Flipping	Asset improvement completed	Buy an asset, increase its value and sell the asset with a profit.	Subject matter expert knowledge about the asset
Buy and maintain	n/a	If you are still making money with your asset, but the value has dropped below your purchase price, consider investing additional money to increase the value and income.	n/a
Buy and Hold	Market price x amount above purchase price	Combination of portfolio and passive income investment.	n/a
Buy to Sell for Profit	Market price x amount above purchase price	Trading transaction. Almost all stock investments fall under this category.	Stop-loss
Strategic investment	Strategic goal achieved	Sometimes it makes sense to buy an asset to improve your market position.	Mergers and acquisitions

Figure 24.1 Investment Strategies Summary

CHAPTER 25

Retirement Assets

"Retirement: It's nice to get out of the rat race, but you have to learn to get along with less cheese."

—Gene Perret

"The challenge of retirement is how to spend time without spending money."

—Author Unknown

"The question isn't at what age I want to retire; it's at what income."

—George Foreman

"There are some who start their retirement long before they stop working."

—Robert Half

These above quotes illustrate very well what different views currently exist on the subject of retirement. Some people see retirement as a point in life where everything changes, and some see retirement as a decade long transition. I observe that the majority of the population today is that retirement begins at a point in time where one stops working and begins to draw from their savings for their living expenses until they die. There is also a very different picture of retirement, which views retirement as a time when one has long passed the point where one's passive income exceeds their expenses. This view sees retirement as a gradual process where one shifts away from earning the majority of one's salary as the only source of income and begins to rely on the income produced from the assets, which one owns. It is my opinion that anybody could achieve financial independence beginning in their twenties or thirties.

Recently, I was talking to a former co-worker. We were chatting about the question when he plans to retire. He stated he would probably need another ten years before he would be able to retire. I asked him why he had picked ten years as his estimate? He answered that he planned to have a certain amount invested in paper assets before considering to retire. He said that he had not reached that figure yet. So, I asked him how much he thought would be enough. Even though he did not give me a concrete number, his intentions were pretty clear to me. His goal was to accumulate an indefinite amount of financial products, which he would then gradually sell after he retired while living on the proceeds. I told him that I thought that this strategy for retirement might prove very risky.

I argued that what he was describing was a *portfolio retirement plan.* His plan does work because, over time, usually under a financial advisor's guidance, the prospective retiree will accumulate various paper assets using the principle of diversity of risk until his portfolio has reached an optimum mix. After retirement, the portfolio requires continual management and is the primary source to cover his living expenses. Assets are gradually sold as needs arise. What investment counselors usually advise is a mixture of growth stocks and high yielding tax-free municipal bonds. The problem is that the portfolio begins to diminish from the very first day of retirement. The control of its value is mostly beyond that of the respective retiree. He is 'bleeding it off,' and he is not in control. Market factors will probably be the determinative causal factor in the ultimate value of his portfolio.

Furthermore, most 401(k) and IRAs retirement plans are based on the accumulation of paper assets. Paper assets are risky because they tend to lose actual purchasing power over time due to inflation. There is also a risk of a potential currency devaluation driven by international economic forces. Besides, these retirement funds are only designed to support retirees and perhaps their spouses when they retire. But most such plans do not make any provision for the couple's children or grandchildren. And finally, these plans are unsustainable because classic retirement plans are only designed to fund a person's life for about a couple of decades. The longer a person lives, the better the chances are of running out of money too soon. I believe that there is a better way:

RETIREMENT PLANNING FOR INCOME

So, why not consider a different retirement plan? A plan that involves increasing your financial literacy and learning how to manage your assets years before you retire. Why not start the path to retirement today? You can do this by smartly downsizing your expenses while simultaneously increasing your financial education toward the point where you can begin living primarily from your passive income rather than your salary or savings?

Many people convert their 401(k) retirement plans to self-directed tax-free retirement accounts, which allow them to invest in all five asset classes: real estate, commodities, businesses, securities, and money markets. This way, they can start creating passive income that goes right back into their retirement account, and they are building a nest egg for their retirement, the residue of which can be passed on to their children.

I converted my 401(k) account to a self-directed retirement account in early 2008, and my retirement fund produces a steady monthly income from the rental of several condominiums. This income goes right back into my retirement account. Of course, since it is a tax-free account, it is designed to support me after my retirement, which I plan to start at the age of 65, I cannot withdraw any money today without paying a financial penalty. There are many companies out there that can help you in converting your retirement plan.

	Portfolio Retirement Planning	Retirement Planning for Income
Income after retirement	Very low or no income. Income is mostly exclusively from funds withdrawing.	Sustainable, medium to high income
Beneficiaries	Mainly only the retiree	Retiree, entire family and all future generations
Risk	Very high risk. The entire risk of money market like inflation, currency fluctuations, recessions, depressions	Lower risk. Income will still come in after retiree passes away.
Time line	Until death of retiree	Throughout generations

Figure 25.1 Advantages of Planning for Income

The following diagram illustrates two paths: the average track and the sophisticated path to a secure and early retirement. The average person with a typical portfolio retirement account in the form of a classic 401(k) plan builds a cushion of savings during his or her employment years, which he or she will draw upon at retirement. A typical retirement planner will ask you one central question: *"what do you want your withdrawal-rate to be when you retire?"* You can challenge your retirement planner by saying you want the withdrawal-rate to be zero. He will explain that this is not possible. But if you prefer that your retirement income comes from income-producing assets, you will need to invest in your financial literacy and investment skills.

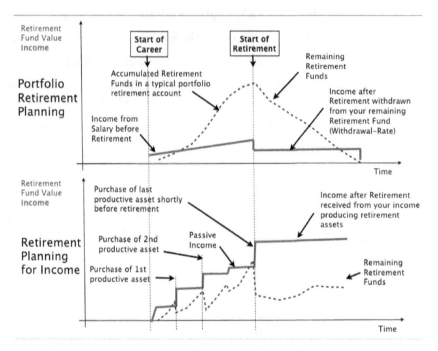

Figure 25.2 Two Ways of Retirement Planning—An Empiric Approach

However, sophisticated investors are investors for income. They use their savings and dedicate their time to the purchase and creation of several income-producing assets. This strategy can provide passive income not only during their working years but also after retirement.

I realize that my retirement approach asks a lot of most people. The message I want to bring across in my book is that it is a lifetime project, and we should ideally initiate it when we are younger.

If you are now in your late 50s or even 60s, this plan might not be feasible. However, if you invest in your financial education, you can teach your children and grandchildren.

CHAPTER 26

Universal Basic Income

"Most Americans agree that technology is going to eliminate many more jobs than it is going to create." —Andrew Yang

Universal Basic Income (UBI) has been proposed and discussed for centuries. The idea of a government-run income goes back to the early 16th century when Sir Thomas More's *Utopia* depicted a society where every person receives a guaranteed income. In the late 18th century, English radical Thomas Spence and American revolutionary Thomas Paine both declared their support for a welfare system that guaranteed all citizens an individual income.

Nineteenth-century debate on basic income was limited, but a basic income called a "state bonus" was widely discussed during the early part of the Twentieth century.

- In 1946, the United Kingdom implemented unconditional family allowances for the second and subsequent children of every family.
- In the 1960s and 1970s, the United States and Canada conducted several experiments with negative income taxation, a related welfare system.
- From the 1980s and onward, the debate in Europe took off more broadly, and since then, it has expanded to many countries around the world.
- A few countries have implemented large-scale welfare systems that have some similarities to basic income, such as Bolsa

Família in Brazil. From 2008 onward, several experiments with basic income and related systems have taken place.

- In 2020, Andrew Yang launched Humanity Forward, a non-profit that bolsters UBI.

ARE WE READY FOR BASIC UNIVERSAL INCOME?

The short answer is no; we are not ready. Results from several test groups receiving Universal Basic Income (UBI) each month show that the most fundamental concept of life has not changed for participants at all, and that is the question: what do people do with their lives?

To me, UBI is like the classic example of *giving fish to the hungry instead of teaching them how to fish*. It seems to me that we cannot buy people's creativity or sophistication with money. We also cannot force sophistication and creativity onto people. I propose that Universal Basic Income has to grow from within, from the ground up. With artificial intelligence taking more and more skilled labor jobs, this book can help us get inspired by and interested in subjects like Generational Wealth. Instead of giving us a false sense of security by receiving free money, we might want to find out how to best invest in our future after realizing that finding employment is no longer an option.

CHAPTER 27

Asset Ownership and Control

One day, my six-year-old son discovered a cute white teddy bear that I used to play with when I was a child. I have owned that teddy bear for my whole life. I remember when my grandmother gave it to me as a present when I turned six myself. My son fell in love with my little teddy bear, asking me if he could keep it. I said it would be alright if he played with it but that I would like to keep it.

My son disagreed and immediately said: "No, I want to have it forever." In other words, he wanted to own the teddy bear. Playing with it for the day was not enough for him. He wanted to own it. When I told my son he could play with it as long as he wanted to, my son protested and said he wanted it to be his. He repeated that he wanted to own the bear. So, I gave up. I said, "Okay, it is yours, then." But I told him, even though he would now own the bear, I would say to him when he can play with it and when he couldn't. To my surprise, he was immediately fine with that arrangement. He just wanted to be able to say that he owned it.

I suddenly realized that ownership must be something exceptional. So, I began to ask myself, "Why do people like to be able to claim ownership?" What does ownership mean? So I looked into the concept of ownership and control a little further.

OWNERSHIP VERSUS CONTROL

I realized that asset ownership and asset control are two different things. At one extreme, you can own something but have no control over it. An example is the case of a limited partnership. The limited partners have an equity interest in the company but do not have the right to exercise management control of the business. In other cases, people may have control over an asset, but they do not own it. An example would be an agency relationship where the principal has entrusted you with sole discretion to manage his asset.

The case of common stockholders provides another example of asset ownership and control. A holder of a share of common stock in a company has voting rights but does not exercise actual direct control over the management decisions of the company, the board of directors does.

In other words, it is common for one person to control an asset, while another person reaps the asset's benefits. I further noticed that the English language seems to be vague in the meaning of ownership. The German language has two different words, which clearly distinguish between property ownership as 'Eigentum' and the possession as 'Besitz.' The English dictionary seems to be more flexible in this regard.

A very different example is that of the case of homeowners. A lender is usually the legal owner of the property if the owner took a loan to purchase the property. The value of the home is the assurance that the purchaser will probably continue to make the mortgage payments during the period of the loan until the house is paid off.

The legal possessor retains the right to redemption. The homeowner has the right to live in the home and use it. A title to an asset is recognized as ownership by law. If you have not paid off the house you live in, your payments might be construed as a type of rent. The only difference is that you are credited with the payment as equity, whereas in the rental agreement, you do not accumulate equity in your home.

I recommend that you invest the time to check your records to see if you find the original deed for your home. If you still have a mortgage on your house, your bank will probably have the original title.

What about other asset ownership examples? Do you have the freedom that you imagined would be yours as the ultimate owner of an asset?

Let us take the example of your position as a citizen of the United States. Do the citizens own the country, or does the country's government own their citizens?

Were you aware that we, as taxpayers, could be considered as government assets? It may sound extreme to say this, but, from a financial perspective, the citizens make up the most significant source of the revenue stream to the government. We pay ten times more money to the government as income tax than all companies in the United States combined. So, we are precious assets to the government. Of course, you could also argue that we pay the government with your tax dollars to do its job. However, if you think about it, we do not pay the government with money that we own, we pay the government with the time we spend working to earn the salary we pay taxes from.

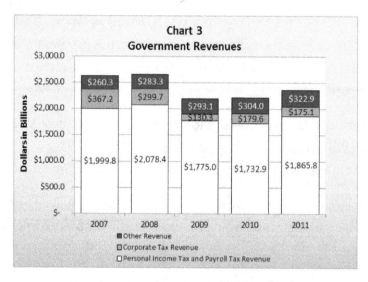

Figure 27.1 Government Revenues on www.fms.treas.gov

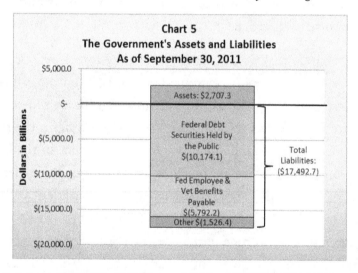

Figure 27.2 Government's Assets and Liabilities on www.fms.treas.gov

What about the company you work for? Are you an asset to your employer? You bet! What about your house? Whose asset is that? Your home is generating income, yes, but not for you–for the bank. The most basic explanation of an asset that we own is: assets are things that we own and which we benefit from financially.

Let us return now to the example of my son. Any time he wants to play with 'his' bear, he had to ask me if he could do so. Now, ask yourself if there are any restrictions on your use and benefits derived from 'your' assets. If you enumerate the real benefits, you will see who the ultimate beneficiaries are, and you will see who owns your assets.

CHAPTER 28

Economic Progress for Generations

"I don't want a nation of thinkers. I want a nation of workers."
—John D. Rockefeller

How can a sophisticated investor leave wealth for generations and measure their actual economic progress over time?

Wouldn't it be wonderful if we could find a way to measure a family's financial success and compare it with other families? Adam Smith did something very similar when he tried to explain why some countries are wealthier than others in his classic work, *The Wealth of Nations.* He concluded that the most prosperous nations were not countries such as Spain with the most extensive access to silver and gold but rather the mercantile nations such as England and France. Through extensive international trade and the beginning of manufacturing on an industrial scale, they were accumulating far more wealth than countries that sold their natural resources. Today, we understand this concept better, but that was not the case at the time the hunt still dominated the race for colonies for gold and silver.

Very recently, an economist named *Thomas Piketty* has developed a formula that explains in great detail the relative financial health of nations. By reading his book *Capital* recently, I realized that we also need to apply this formula to our individual financial situation.

Thomas Piketty is a Professor at the Paris School of Economics. In 2014, he published his book entitled *Capital in the Twenty-First Century*. Piketty published what he calls his *First Fundamental Law of Capitalism*. Thomas Piketty analyzed economic data like national assets, national income, and the financial return on capital from many countries going back many centuries. He has developed what is, in my opinion, a basic formula like Albert Einstein's relativity theory. I believe what Albert Einstein has achieved for physics, Thomas Piketty has written for economics. In Thomas Piketty's formula, only three components determine the success of a country's economic progress. These components are:

- The sum of all assets a country owns,
- The total annual national income and,
- The annual rate of return from all assets.

The formula is as follows: $\alpha = r \times \beta$

Which reads:

α = (return on capital) x (*capital/income* ratio)

Whereas:

β = capital divided by total income

r = return from all capital (assets)

Piketty's formula reveals that countries that receive high returns (r) on their national assets like manufacturing businesses are far more successful than countries that are only selling their assets like their natural resources and thus depleting their wealth over time.

Based on Thomas Piketty's extensive analysis, he concludes that a country typically achieves value for α of about 0.3 or 30%. Very successful countries like Germany and France, make an even higher α, whereas economically challenged countries, such as North Africa, reach α of far less than 0.2 (20%).

For almost 250 years, since Adam Smith, nations' economic success seemed more important than individuals, families, and generations' financial success. I believe that societies can only prosper when the average family's financial success is better or as successful as national success. Therefore, I stress the importance of using Piketty's formula to measure families, generations, and small businesses' economic progress and prosperity. When we plug in salaries, capital income, and assets owned by average families in America today, we find very different values for α than the ones Piketty finds for counties.

Most families don't even have any passive income (income received from capital), so r is zero, which means α is also zero. Even families with a small return on their assets will mostly only reach values for $\boxtimes$ less than 0.01. Please refer to Appendix A for a detailed analysis of values for α of families with very different financial backgrounds. You can also plug in your personal or your family's total salary, return on all your investments, and the combined value of your assets. You might discover very quickly that your financial situation is quite alarming. In that case, I encourage you to learn how to become a more sophisticated investor.

CHAPTER 29

Evaluating your Home as an Asset

*Is there a difference between your buying a home
and investing in real estate?*

How much do you pay each month to live in your house? If you pay to live in your home, your house is an expense item in your budget, not an asset. In his book entitled Rich Dad Poor Dad, Robert Kiyosaki says: *"If you stop working today, an asset puts money in your pocket, and a liability takes money from your pocket. Too often, people call liabilities assets. It's important to know the difference between the two."*

Robert Kiyosaki is referring to the concept illustrated by the asset quadrants. In the grid, you see the two dimensions income and value. We are all too focused on asset value and not on asset income. The house you live in is either a young cow or a dead cow. It will never be a cash cow or not even an old cow.

We, as a society, got used to specific language that makes us feel good. *'Life is good'* is one of them. *'Homeownership'* is another. Officially, we might use the house as if we owned it, but it is only a form of rent we pay for a long time. The word mortgage comes from the French words mort, which means 'dead' and the word *'gage'* means *'pledge.'* The house we live in is just another consumer toy that we have to pay for each month. It is risky to hope or speculate on selling the house later with a profit. But did you buy your home in the first place to make money? Even if you rent out parts of your house to tenants, your house is still not an asset. Even if you outright own your home without any mortgage, that house is still no asset since you have to pay taxes, maintenance, and other costs.

So, you typically will not generate any income when you buy a house you intend to live in. Instead, it is an expense. Most people focus only on their house's financial value; they look at only one dimension of the asset quadrant diagram: the vertical asset value axis. They are traders. Traders are *one-dimensional* investors. They try to buy low, and their goal is to sell high.

THE RIGHT DOWN PAYMENT

A home is a residential property, which you and your family intend to live in. It is not an investment. It is an expense item like your car or any other item you use. But when you buy your home, you will have to apply some investor thinking to reduce financial risks.

If you intend to buy a home, for example, for 228,000 dollars, take a loan of 200,000 dollars and put down 28,000 dollars, you will pay at current low rates of 5% about 1,200 dollars a month for a 30-year mortgage plus other monthly costs like taxes and maintenance. Let's assume that that property shows a rent estimate between 1,200 and 1,600 dollars. You can find out rent estimates on many popular websites like zillow.com.

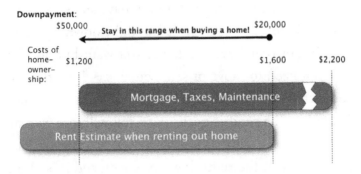

Figure 29.1 Calculation for the right down payment for your home

If you do the math, you can determine a range for your down payment, which allows your monthly costs to stay below the amount you would rent out for. Then you have the freedom to move somewhere else, start renting the place out and receive a monthly income. Whereas if you financed as in this example more than 200,000 dollars, you might have to pay some money each month when you rent it out because the mortgage would be higher than you will receive.

WHAT ABOUT REMODELING?

What about upgrading your house with new energy-saving appliances, new windows, or a new heat pump? Remodeling your home can lower your expenses and might increase the value of the house. It could save you a lot of money, but it would not make you any money. Your home is still an expense.

EXIT STRATEGIES

Every investor will need to plan for an exit strategy. And you, as a homebuyer, should do the same thing before buying your home. It is for the case when the unforeseeable happens: imagine the price of your home drops below the amount you owe the bank, and you need to move out of state due to a job change, or as many people, you get divorced and need to sell the home.

So, when you buy a home, make sure you have an exit strategy. One way to do so is to get a loan with the right down payment. That way, you will not only have the home you want but also have insurance if you need to move or sell. You always have the option to move somewhere else because you can either sell your home with a profit if the housing market goes up, or you will receive a monthly income by renting it out if it is underwater. You cannot lose when buying a home with the right down payment, and it is also a good compromise between being a homeowner and an investor. It would help if you never considered your home to be an investment, but you still have to crunch some numbers to lower the financial risks. By planning for the right down payment, you will reduce the risk of financial loss or default dramatically. It will likely prevent you from going through a short-sale procedure or foreclosure, significantly impacting your credit score.

When you purchase your home, please do your homework and calculate the right amount for your down payment and stick to it. Even if banks allow a lower down payment or you would like to go for the bigger, more expensive home, stick to your plan. A higher down payment increases your payment upfront, and you might not buy the house you want. But the right down payment will save you from massive trouble in the future.

Remember: The job of mortgage brokers is to sell loans. So, if you ask them whether they can give you a home loan, they will say *'sure,'* and they will try to make it work for them. But be careful! Before you sign, make sure it will work for you, too!

CHAPTER 30

Your Continued Action Plan

"Stay hungry, stay foolish!"—Steve Jobs

The proper amount of the following three ingredients is required to build wealth for generations: your *passive income*, your *financial literacy* (sophistication of your mind), your *expenses*. This section will tell you how to manage these three components.

The transition from an average investor to a sophisticated investor will not happen overnight. You recall our formula for wealth calculation: W = P (Passive Income) over the sum of E (Expenses) and P: $W = P/(P+E)$. When W is greater than 0.5, I consider you to be a sophisticated investor because you can cover all your personal expenses with passive income, so you have time to manage your capital. It may take you ten years or more to reach W=0.5 if you start from zero. I know that patience will pay off. It often takes time to shift your paradigms, and it certainly is a life-changing process. But it can also be fun and exciting to explore new opportunities. You will eventually look back and ask yourself: *"how could I ever have lived differently?"*

The primary goal of a successful investor is to increase his or her wealth W to be higher than 0.5.

If your wealth W score is lower than 0.5, you will still need a salary to pay for your expenses, such as rent or the mortgage on your home. To help become a sophisticated investor faster, you can lower your costs of living or boost your passive income, or do both simultaneously. But merely working harder to improve your salary S will not increase your wealth as we have defined wealth W. Being wealthy is the ability to acquire assets that can produce passive income. Increasing your salary S with a non-investor mind might only raise your temptation to increase your expenditures now that your new salary level has conveyed a sense of security to you. Our goal is to acquire wealth that you can pass on to future generations. And the wealth of this magnitude is unlikely to emerge from salary increases. Raising your passive income P will increase your independence and your overall wealth.

We are facing massive challenges in the world today due to the increasing gap between rich and poor. Based on a document presented by G. William Domhoff of the UC-Santa Cruz Sociology Department, Wealth, Income, and Power, the top 1% of Americans own 34.6% of America's wealth. This wealth comes in the form of factories, land, major retail outlets, and other productive assets in the nation. Have you wondered which jobs people in this 1% bracket have? Owning such kind of wealth, what are the odds that they have regular jobs at all? Is it not far more likely that they serve on boards of directors or as principal officers in corporations? Could they possibly balance the maintenance of such large portfolios and still have time to work for money a 40-hour week? This thought explains why real wealth depends upon passive income. But the story gets worse because the next 4% controls 27.3% of all the nation's wealth. By adding these figures together, the top 5% owns 61.9%. These numbers mean that the top 5% of Americans control over half of the nation's wealth. Not to belabor this point, we will not consider each segment of the pie, but I will conclude my top end by stating that the top 10% of Americans control 73.1% of the nation's wealth, almost ¾ of the nation's wealth. This number means that the 90% must get by on the remaining quarter 25%. But now I will tell you a fact so startling that you may hardly believe it: the bottom 40% of Americans must get by with only 0.2% of the nation's wealth. How do these people differ from the peasants of the old feudal days? Yet, the bottom 40% performs most of the labor, which keeps the lights on, and the wheel spinning.

What is happening? The only way to improve this situation is to raise the investor sophistication of everyone to increase checks-and-balances between the ordinary people and *The Elite*. Would you agree? The higher the gap between *The Elite* and the ordinary people, the higher is the risk of the rise of tyranny and undemocratic behavior in the ruling elite. Many people are frustrated with the current wealth gap. At this time, available investment products seem to be under the control of a small minority. The rich are getting wealthier, and all the rest of us are getting relatively more impoverished by the day.

Have you asked yourself where you should put your hard-earned savings without the fear of the erosion of values and the fear of high taxes, maintenance costs, and inflation will eat into your meager savings? Do you feel that you are only being taken advantage of by The Elite's big investor machinery? You may worry that your future retirement funds may prove inadequate because of the ever-decreasing buying power of the dollar? As an average investor, it is time to wake up and build your independent financial foundation.

The times have changed since the dawn of the new century. Natural resources are becoming scarcer and economic growth is increasingly *independent* of new job creation.

The Massachusetts Institute of Technology MIT published a fascinating e-book about how information technologies affect jobs, skills, wages, and the economy. If you hope that the old boom times will return soon, you should think twice about it. Many reputable economists, former CEO's and politicians are screaming already from the rooftops: the times of endless economic growth based on skilled labor and cheap resources are over. A mega long-term *Kondratieff Shift* is underway. With automation and artificial intelligence taking gradually away skilled labor jobs, everybody who wants to maintain their lifestyle will have to rely increasingly on their creativity, sophistication, and financial assets. This book provides some of the knowledge and tools to get you started to be a sophisticated investor on levels five and six. You should take action today and develop a 10-year plan if you wish to become financially free. Consider the following steps:

- *First*, start increasing your own and your family's financial literacy by learning how to spend smarter and decrease your expenses.
- *Second*, try to continuously improve your financial education by researching all asset classes even if they are beyond your own current ability to purchase them. By doing this, you will develop a habit of thinking through potential opportunities so that you will be ready to strike when you can afford them.
- *Third*, when you do invest, try to avoid merely paper assets. Instead, try to purchase income-generating assets. Use paper assets to store capital on short-term bases while you research better opportunities.
- *Fourth*, by doing the first three steps, you will gradually supplement your salary with passive income, which means you will be progressively becoming wealthier.
- *Fifth*, when your passive income becomes higher than your expenses, you may find it possible to devote most of your time managing your investments. You may even decide to stop working for someone else.

- *Sixth*, at this point, your assets will be your new "job", and the distinction between your passive income and your salary will cease to exist.

Another way to look at these six steps is to look at it from the analogy of your progression through school grades. You might discover that you are already in a particular school grade. Then try to complete all your school grades presented below and finish in college.

Kindergarten: analogy to unemployed or being on welfare.

Elementary School:

School Grade	Goals for Financial Sophistication's in analogy to school grade
1st Grade	You have a job and a small salary.
2nd Grade	You have a job that pays enough so you have a checking and savings account.
3rd Grade	You get your first credit card.
4th Grade	You develop financial habits.
5th Grade	You begin to research personal financial management.

Middle School:

Grade	Goals for Financial Sophistication's in analogy to school grade
6th Grade	You begin to explore real-life options in your community where you can begin to hear about investment opportunities.
7th Grade	Set investment goals for the next three years.
8th Grade	You purchase your first passive income-producing asset.

High School:

9th Grade	You stop working for money and you live from your passive income. You start working with other investors.
10th Grade	You form partnerships and create financial products.
11th Grade	You become a mentor for others and for your employees.
12th Grade	You focus on graduating as sophisticated investor.

College:

Year	Goals for Financial Sophistication's in analogy to college semesters.
1st	You take a complete inventory of all your assets and re-evaluate them.
2nd	You reposition all your assets so that they deliver the best returns for all partners involved.
3rd	You study and practice ways how to give back. You plan the generational succession by involving all family members in your quest for what is right and wrong, your pursuit for knowledge, and your interest in acquiring new assets. You read books like "Family Wealth" by James E. Hughes Jr. to plan for the future.
4th	Your primary focus on becoming a patron to others. You graduate as a philanthropist.

Fig 30.1 Alternative School Grades

I hope this book has given you some ideas for how you can change your life to become a financially free and independent person and build wealth for generations. By doing so, you can not only free yourself, but you will also give your children and even their children leverage, so they don't have to sell their time and efforts in the market place.

The following chapter is dedicated to my grandfather, who was a financial auditor and assistant professor for economics at a Swedish college in the 1930s.

CHAPTER 31

Family Wealth—My Grandfather's Story

Ingemar Aae, my paternal grandfather, was born in Linköping, Sweden, on June 9, 1909. He studied at the then newly inaugurated College of Economics in Stockholm HHS, Härnösand, from 1927 to 1930. He graduated with a business degree and started to work as a primary assistant for Professor Oskar K. G. Sillén, who was the key figure who brought business auditing to life in Sweden and is known as "the true creator of the modern audit system."

My story of Ingemar's life begins on September 23, 1935. A large ocean liner was anchored in the harbor of Gothenburg, a seaport in southwestern Sweden, on the Kattegat strait. The ship was scheduled to leave Sweden at noon on that day, heading to New York.

Earlier that morning, my grandfather, a slim five foot ten inch tall twenty-six year old fellow with dark hair and blue eyes named Ingemar Aae, woke up precisely at five o'clock that morning to make last preparations for his journey to America. He was invited by the American Scandinavian Foundation to study and work in the field of accounting as an auditor and revisor in Chicago, Illinois. His immigration papers had already been issued on August 23, 1935, so he was ready to start his journey to America.

It was an inauspicious time for new beginnings. Depression had already shown its effects around the world. Unemployment in America had hovered at a rate of between fifteen and twenty percent for years. President Franklin D. Roosevelt initiated a series of governmental programs called the New Deal in 1933. They had proven to be only moderately successful. In the end, they had failed to improve the overall employment situation. The second phase of the New Deal was intended to replace many programs of initial New Deal legislation from 1934 to 1936. This second New Deal had succeeded in improving the economy, starting in the year of 1937.

Amid all this economic and social turmoil, Ingemar was determined to contribute personally to the overall economic recovery by auditing businesses and verifying that companies complied with the new regulations.

At around eight o'clock on the morning of his departure from his former home, Ingemar had breakfast with his fiancé Marta Söderholtz. Ingemar's parents Gustav and Karin Aae came at eight-thirty to wish him all the best for his trip. His mother handed him a brand new photo camera, and she told him to take many pictures to show them the places he went to in the modern world of America.

Accompanied by Marta and his parents, Ingemar arrived at the ship named S.S. GRIPSHOLM at eleven a.m. He enjoyed the exclusive interior design in the ship and the friendly personnel that helped him on deck to find his cabin. The trip to his new country was relaxing but uneventful. After five days, the ship arrived at the Port of New York. Following the immigration procedures, Ingemar spent some time in New York City, and downtown Manhattan visited the Niagara Falls in upstate New York.

He then continued his journey to Illinois. On Sunday, October 6th, 1935, Ingemar arrived in Chicago by train. The American Scandinavian Foundation rented a small room near the Field Building at 127 West Upper Wacker Drive, Chicago, Illinois. He arrived weary but determined early on a Sunday morning at the Chicago Union Station after a long twenty-hour train ride through the beautiful countryside areas that border Lake Erie.

After having lunch at a small diner in the neighborhood, Ingemar checked out Chicago's busy downtown areas on foot. He was already mentally preparing for his new work in the Field Building, where his new employer Ernst & Young, was located.

Figure 31.1 Ingemar Aae in Chicago, in September 1935 (private photo)

On Monday, October 7th, 1935, Ingemar was scheduled to meet the secretary of the office at 8:00 AM for an office introductory tour and meet the director of the auditing department.

The director welcomed Ingemar and cut right to the chase: "the catastrophic destabilization of unregulated banking and financial markets threatened to destroy many national economies worldwide.

Roosevelt's administration had already taken drastic measures to correct the problem, such as closing all banks for a 'bank holiday' and only allowing them to re-open after they had proven that they were, in fact, solvent or reasonably so. This action had worked to stabilize the banking sector of the economy. Besides, the creation of the Federal Deposit Insurance Corporation, or FDIC, was part of the First New Deal initiative to restore investor confidence."

Ingemar used a short pause in the discussion to comment, *"I have read about President Roosevelt and the New Deal while still in Sweden, and I am here in the United States to learn more about the New Deal and to help wherever I can. What do you wish me to do?"*

The director answered, "Well, we need you to work with our teams to help companies create adequate financial reports, especially regarding their employees. Mr. Roosevelt's radical approaches to banking and unemployment have resulted in many opponents labeling him socialist. Still, millions of unemployed Americans have found work as a result of the New Deal programs. Some programs, such as the Civil Works Administration and the Public Works Administration, have hired workers directly rather than waiting for other employer incentives to take effect. The Civilian Conservation Corps has hired many unemployed men to clean and maintain our national forests and parklands. Your spirit is in tune with the national recovery effort. So, Ingemar, I am glad you are here. We need to make sure that companies implement and follow the new New Deal rules. That's how you can best contribute. I was hoping you could learn about the new rules and then go out to our clients and work with our team to audit their accounting books. These companies have already started many projects voluntarily to establish internal auditing departments that perform regular inspections in all of their departments, but they have a long way to go. You may begin at once."

Figure 31.2 The Field Building in Chicago, Illinois painted by Sehnten Wanjord
(Author's family collection)

Ingemar was glad to learn first-hand that his efforts would be needed. He instantly replied in Swedish: "Ja visst!" And he corrected himself immediately and said: "of course, sir."

Ingemar had studied English in school for several years, and his English grades were always satisfactory, so he had no trouble at all understanding and speaking English. However, once in a while, a Swedish saying would slip from his month. His language caused no problems because people were very used to the Swedish language in Illinois at the time. Illinois was full of Swedish immigrants.

Figure 31.3 Original Newspaper article in Svensk-amerikanska historiska sallskapet 1937, Svensk Metallverken

The following morning, Ingemar arrived at the client's site, which was a big factory located several miles out of town. It was a metal manufacturing plant, which had barely survived the Great Depression thus far. But now it was a vital part of the newly emerging automotive industry in Chicago and Detroit.

Ingemar arrived by taxi in a Yellow Cab. The reception area that he entered was cheaply maintained, and Ingemar had difficulty opening the small entrance door, which was about to fall off its hinges. The woman at the front desk proved to be very lovely, but she seemed overwhelmed with her work.

The receptionist guided Ingemar to where the auditing team was located on the first floor in the same part of the building. There were four external consultants and one project manager from the factory. The consultants already had created a project plan that determined what has to be done to set up a new controlling department for the company. The team members introduced Ingemar to the project and assigned him the task of setting up a process for creating and auditing the balance sheets of the factory. The project manager from

Ernst & Young explained, "Before the Wall Street Crash of 1929 there was little regulation of securities. Even firms whose securities were publicly traded published no regular reports or, worse, they included rather misleading reports based on arbitrarily selected data. The Securities Act of 1933 has been enacted to avoid another crash of Wall Street. It requires the disclosure of the balance sheet, profit and loss statement, and the names and compensation amounts of corporate officers in all firms whose securities are publicly traded."

In 1934 the U.S. Securities and Exchange Commission (SEC) was established to regulate the stock market and prevent corporate abuses relating to the sale of securities and corporate reporting. These reports had to be verified by independent auditors, and this is where Ingemar came in.

The project manager asked him, "Can you please work with the accounting team of this factory and create a list of all assets and liabilities? We will transfer them to a standard balance sheet when we are back in our Ernst & Young headquarters in Chicago."

Ingemar was excited to be part of such an important task. Ernst & Young spearheaded a new finance practice that used standard financial reporting for public and private companies. At that time, Ernst & Young's activities were not limited to the auditing, though. They helped companies around the world to establish procedures and departments that would create these new financial reports as standard practices.

Ingemar worked at his initial assignment for six months. When he finished there in March of 1936, he felt that he had not only helped the factory tremendously but also learned so much, with the guidance of his colleagues at Ernst & Young, that he was now a fully competent auditor. Ingemar felt comfortable talking about his experience and the things he had learned when he returned to Stockholm. On March 5, 1936, he arrived in Goteborg on the ship that he had taken the previous year.

The following day after his return, he decided to visit an old professor. When they met in the professor's office in Stockholm, his mentor and new boss, Oskar K. G. Sillén, was already very excited to hear what Ingemar had to say about his trip to America.

It did not take very long until Mr. Sillén asked Ingemar to speak at the University of Stockholm about the new world of auditing in America. My grandfather discussed the necessity and importance of establishing internal processes within companies and accomplishing these reforms within a short time frame.

Revisor Aae i talarstolen.

Figure 31.4 Ingemar Aae Explains the auditing practice in Sweden on Jan 27, 1937 (Newspaper Svensk Dagbladet)

Between 1937 and 1941, Ingemar worked in Professor Sillén's office. He gave several speeches at various locations in Stockholm, including many companies. In these talks, he advised manufacturing companies regarding procedures to implement their internal auditing departments to improve compliance with "modern accounting methods."

In March of 1942, Ingemar was promoted to be Professor Sillén's assistant. He started his new position in downtown Stockholm. There, he wrote a letter to his sister who lived in Southern Sweden:

March 26, 1942

My Dear Sister!

It took some time until I could find the shirt for father. But now I got it, and that is why I am sending this card. Today, I got my own office, and I love to work there. The rest of the family is doing pretty well. My boy has a little cold, but that has obviously no effect on his energy.

The day before yesterday, dad and mom were here to take a bath. They told us about their plans to go on a trip to the countryside. They thought about Källvik, but it seems hotels are all full. I will be dismissed from military service until March 1944, which is very pleasant. Otherwise, there is no more news. I hope you are doing well and that you will get to know friendly people.

All the best,

Your brother Ingemar

When Ingemar wrote this letter to his sister, he did not know that tragedy was about to strike him. Four months after he wrote this letter to his sister, he was diagnosed with leukemia during a routine doctor's visit. The doctor said his white blood cells were noticeably elevated.

It was a wonderful and warm summer in Sweden. Ingemar was at the peak of his young life. He had a happy family and enjoyed his dream career. Now illness might shorten what had been a life of achievement and expectation prematurely.

Due to Sweden's high latitude, one thousand miles north of the U.S. state of Maine, the sun sets very late in summer. The days are long and beautiful there. Ingemar had no choice other than to face this disastrous and sudden change in his family's lives. That entire summer and through the following fall, Ingemar went from one hospital to the next to discover that there was no cure to his developing sickness. He had blood cancer for which no remedy would avail. The days grew quickly shorter; the leaves would be falling soon in October, and grim winter knocked on the door in early November.

In 1942, the winter in Stockholm turned out to be one of the coldest and darkest winters in memory. But throughout all of those months, Ingemar did not lose faith, although he got progressively weaker each day. He had been diagnosed with Acute Lymphatic Leukemia, which leaves its victims very little time to realize what is happening to them.

Early in January 1943, Ingemar developed a high fever, had night sweats, headaches, easy bruising and bleeding, bone and joint pain, a swollen and painful belly from an enlarged spleen, and most of the time, he felt exhausted and weak. He had already lost thirty pounds by the end of December 1942, and by February of 1943, he was forced by his illness to stop working for Professor Sillén.

It was a Saturday morning, April 17, 1943. A late winter cold front had reached Stockholm during the night and covered Stockholm in a thick snow and ice layer. Ingemar had been admitted to the Sabbatsbergs hospital in downtown Stockholm. That Saturday morning, Ingemar barely woke up at all. Even with a high dose of morphine,

Ingemar must have felt more pain in his joints than ever, and his clothes were soaking wet. He had not eaten for many days at that time. In the last couple of days, Ingemar had been put on a morphine IV, which helped him with his pain and general discomfort. Ingemar was barely conscious, and on Friday, April 16, the doctor notified his wife Marta that his organs were starting to 'shut down.' Marta's sadness and desperateness overshadowed everything else in her life. The only comfort she had was that Ingemar seemed very restful and at peace during these last days.

At 8:00 AM on Saturday, April 17, 1943, the nurse came into Ingemar's room to check on her patient. Marta had stayed with Ingemar for the entire night, and at 8:00 AM, she was still asleep holding Ingemar's hand. Immediately, the nurse noticed that Ingemar was awake but seemed to be drifting away. While she was calling the doctor to request further aid, Ingemar stopped breathing. At 9:14 AM, the doctor announced that Ingemar was dead. My grandfather died at the young age of 33.

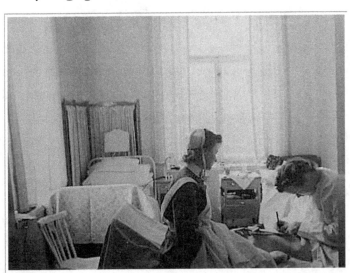

Figure 31.5 Ingemar Aae died on April 17, 1934 in the Sabbatsbergs hospital (private family picture)

A column in the Stockholm newspaper reported in his obituary that on April 17, 1943, the certified auditor, Ingemar Aae, had died in the Sabbatsbergs sjukhus hospital at the age of only 33 years after several months of suffering from a severe illness. He had been the only son of lector Gustav Aae and his wife Karin Aae, whose maiden name was Söderbaum. He left behind his young wife Marta, a three-year-old son, and three sisters: Inga, Margit, and Brita.

On the second day of the Easter celebrations in Stockholm, Ingemar was buried in the Norra Crematorium. His close relatives and friends and many representatives from the companies that Ingemar had worked with and his mentor Professor Sillén joined the service. He gave a moving speech and said that Ingemar had always demonstrated a high degree of talent and dedication for his future profession as an auditor, even during his college studies. He noted that Ingemar had graduated with honors. Ingemar Aae left behind many memories and had been a good husband and father to his family. Relatives and friends gave all their sympathy and will always keep him in their minds.

Ingemar's sudden and early death shattered the life of Ingemar's r wife Marta and his 3-year old son. Ingemar's parents Gustav and Karin Aae had lost a wonderful son. Marta never recovered from the shock of her husband's tragic death. To cope with her sorrow, she withdrew from her regular life. Fortunately, their son grew up and finished college and married a young lady from Germany. Their marriage resulted in three children, of which I am the oldest.

This true story of Ingemar Aae is the story of my grandfather. All events and places are based on family lore and actual records that my family has kept alive for two generations. Some dialog is imaginary, but it reflects what really must have happened.

In reflecting on my grandfather's life, I realized that the time between 1935 and 1943 is very relevant to what still happens today. Although this book is not about auditing and not about the overall economy or government regulations, the achievement of personal wealth still has a lot to do with the financial rules in place at any given historical period. Without learning about these rules of investment, one cannot build wealth.

I realized that investing is really about learning how capitalism operates in a globalized world in the 21st Century. If you wish to build wealth, you must understand regulations and rules in your field of investment and in more general areas like tax regulations and company internal management procedures and structures. I agree with Thomas Piketty's conclusion to his monumental book entitled *Capital in the 21st Century* that democracy depends upon transparency. That way, we, as ordinary citizens, can understand the inner workings of major corporations. But I strongly oppose Piketty's approach to calling for extensive corporate regulations and limitations to put a ceiling on their possibilities to grow. Instead, I propose that average investors become more sophisticated to make independent financial decisions instead of buying canned financial products like mutual funds, company stocks, or bonds from the same organizations that need to we wish to regulate in the first place.

My conviction is that societies can never distribute wealth adequately, and wealth will never trickle down. There is no such thing as a trickle-down economy, to paraphrase Will Rogers, the famous humorist of the 1920s and 1930s. I try to make the point in my book that wealth always flows up. The reason for my view is because marginal increases in wealth are generally leveraged more efficiently by people in the higher investor classes than by average investors or everyday consumers.

This book lays out how to build wealth over time by investing in productive assets. I would like to see the wealth built from the bottom up to limit and regulate wealth at the top. It is my way of seeking to reexamine my grandfather's efforts to regulate, control and audit larger companies.

Literature References

Books serve humankind as an invaluable source of knowledge to feed the minds and propel generational wealth. My book would not have been possible without my in-depth study of previously written literature written by brilliant brains who left us a precious legacy. Here are the most influential books that prelude this work:

The Wealth of Nations—**Adam Smith (5th June 1723–17th July 1790), British Economist, Philosopher, and Author**

The Wealth of Generations–With Special Attention to the Millennials—**The Brookings Institution (brookings.edu)**

Capital in the Twenty-First Century—**Thomas Piketty, French Economist and Professor**

Rich Dad Poor Dad–What the Rich Teach Their Kids About Money That the Poor and Middle Class Do Not!—**Robert Kiyosaki, Best-selling Author of Rich Dad Poor Dad**

The War on Normal People—**Andrew Yang, Entrepreneur, former Presidential Candidate**

How much is enough?—**Robert Skideslsky, Emeritus Professor Political Economy, University of Warwick**

Spending Your Way to Wealth—**Paul Heys, Founding Bank Director, VP Smith Barney**

EmPower Us!, From Crisis to Strategic Harmony—**Ira Kaufman, Velimir Srića**

The Common Good—**Robert B. Reich, American Economic Advisor, Professor, Author, and Political Commentator**

Family Wealth–Keeping it in the Family—**James E. Hughes Jr. (jamesehughes.com)**

The Singularity Is Near, When Humans Transcend Biology—**Ray Kurzweil, American Inventor and Futurist**

The Seven Spiritual Laws of Success: A Practical Guide to the Fulfillment of Your Dreams—**Deepak Chopra, MD, FACP, founder of The Chopra Foundation**

One Thousand Ways to Make Money—**Page Fox 1937**

APPENDIX A

A person's wealth is determined by his ability to acquire new assets without sacrificing his capabilities to cover his expenditures.

In 2013, Thomas Piketty published his best-selling book entitled *Capital in the 21st Century*, in which he introduces two laws. The first law defines α, the capital share of a nation's income. Picketty has drawn worldwide attention with the statement that the disparity between wage earners and capital owners is increasing and that governments should intervene to bring this process to a halt.

The first law is the definition for the capital's share of output α:

$\alpha = r \times \beta$

with r being the net rate of return from capital, and

β = Total Capital (C) / Total Income (I) = C/I.

Piketty's research revealed that a typical α for countries is around 0.3 or 30%.

The following text will illustrate that α for families looks very different compared to α for nations. Let's assume the financial situation of family A is as follows:

- Their Capital C = $100,000 (cash, stocks, incl. residence)
- Total Income I = $50,000 (from salaries + capital returns)
- r = 1% (capital return is 1% of $100,000=$1,000)

Then: α = r x β = 0.01 x ($100,000 / $50,000)=*0.02 or* **2%**

α for this family A is compared to the typical α of countries drastically lower. α of 0.03 is only a fraction of a national α. So, is family A just a bad example or a family with terrible financial management?

Their return on capital in this example is the best-case scenario for an average family and with 1,000$ (1% from 100,000$) not achieved by most families. An average family has typically very little financial capital and receives none to very low return on capital. In case a family has zero return on their capital, which in my observation is rather the norm than the exception, α for this family would be zero. As a reminder, Thomas Piketty's analysis on the other hand reveals that a typical α for countries or nations is around 0.3.

This simple equation tells a story. It proves that nations have managed to be financially successful over time, whereas individuals and generations of families have typically not. It now becomes clear that governments have successfully applied Adam Smith's economic theory described in his book The Wealth of Nations and made nations rich. In contrast, citizens and their generations have been left in the financial Dark Age.

So, how should the numbers look like for a financially successful family? Let us look at family B with the following financial data:

- Capital C = $1,000,000 (net assets, incl. residence)
- Income I = $50,000 (salary, wages, capital return)
- r = 2% (capital return is 2% of $1,000,000=$20,000)

Then: α = r x β = 0.02 x (1,000,000$/50,000$) = *0.4 or 40%*

This family with α of 40% has the same income of 50,000$ as family A and a slightly higher return on their capital. But due to their higher net worth their α is considerably better than the one of the first family. Also, the return from their capital is 20,000$ (2% from 1,000,000$), a considerably higher amount than in the case of family A.

But a family does not need to own much capital to have a high α as demonstrated in example for family C:

- Capital C = 100,000$ (net assets, incl. residence)
- Income I = 50,000$ (salary, wages, capital return)
- r = 20% (capital return is 20% of $100,000=$20,000)

Then: α = r x β = 0.20 x (100,000$/50,000$) = *0.4 or 40%*

Family C has the same value for α since this family can receive 20,000$ (20% from 100,000$) return from its much lower capital base of just 100,000$. The family wealth manager(s) have done a much better job of investing the family capital than family B and A.

Which family do you believe has a higher chance of building wealth for generations? Family A, B, or C?

Let us conclude:

Family	Capital	Return	Income	α
A	100K$	1%	50,000$	0.02
B	1M$	2%	50,000$	0.4
C	100K$	20%	50,000$	0.4

Figure A.1 α for three different families

Family A has the absolutes lowest value for α; in other words, family A is financially absolutely dependent on their earned income. Family B and C have the same α. Still, they are financially in a very different situation since family C seems to have a superior financial education and receive much higher passive income from their capital than family B. Members of family B might represent the lucky heirs of a wealthy relative or are happy lottery winners. Members of family B seem to be financially relatively illiterate, and their expenses will hence eat up all their capital over time.

However, the value for α of both families B and C are comparable to the α of most countries, and both have a great chance of building wealth for generations. I encourage you to find the financial numbers that represent your family and plug them into the formula.

AN EXTREME SITUATION

The following scenario might look somewhat strange to the reader:

- Capital C = 10,000$ (net assets)
- Income I = 10,000$ (salary, wages, capital return)
- r = 100% (returns from all assets)

Then: $\alpha = r \times \beta = 1 \times (10,000\$/10,000\$) = $ *1.0 or 100%*

A value for α of 1.0 or 100% is the perfect financial situation. Imagine that you have 10,000$, which you lend to a friend in London for one year. You have no expenses while you live on a south-sea island, and when you come back to London after that year, your friend was able to start a successful business and pay you back 20,000$. You received a 100% return on your capital while having no expenses. While this scenario is highly unrealistic, this example suggests that you should always try to lower your cost of living and invest your money in the best way possible based on this first fundamental law of capitalism. Reducing costs is a good budgeting practice, and every investor should master it.

Please note:

- Income of a family is considered to be net income (net income = earned income − living expenses + passive income − investment related expenses)
- Capital is the total value of all assets minus all debts associated with these assets (net assets).
- Return r reflects income from capital returns only.
- Income is money received from labor as salary, wages, government and company retirement income, plus income from capital returns.
- Return r is only the monetary return in the form of income from capital and not theoretical income from capital appreciation if assets are sold (capital gains).
- The value for α always falls between 0 and 1 (except for the case when capital returns are negative and the earned income is higher than the losses from capital. In this case, α is negative and the outcome is a financial disaster.
- The higher α is, the better is the financial situation for the entity measured (country or individual).
- All calculations in this book are based on annual financial data.

About the Author

Ingemar Anderson is a trained economist with a Master's Degree in Finance. He is an entrepreneur at heart, book author, speaker, consultant, investor, human-centered capitalist, executive advisor for 25+ years.

Mr. Anderson has started several successful businesses and has invested in many real estate properties for income. His passion for ethical wealth development shows in every part of his life and in this book before you.

To contact the author, please visit his website:

ingemar-anderson.com